Culture Critique

NEW WORLD PERSPECTIVES

General Editors *Arthur and Marilouise Kroker*

Critical explorations of the key thinkers in the New World. Intersecting biography and history, individual monographs in *New World Perspectives* examine the central intellectual vision of leading contributors to politics, culture and society. *New World Perspectives* focus on decisive figures across the broad spectrum of contemporary discourse in art, literature and thought, each in the context of their relationship to the social movements of their times. Moving between the historically specific and the culturally universal, the series as a whole is intended to be both a celebration of the uniqueness of New World thought and a critical appraisal of its most dynamic tendencies, past and present.

AVAILABLE

TECHNOLOGY AND THE CANADIAN MIND: INNIS/ McLUHAN/GRANT
Arthur Kroker

NORTHROP FRYE: A VISION OF THE NEW WORLD
David Cook

CULTURE CRITIQUE: FERNAND DUMONT AND NEW QUEBEC SOCIOLOGY
Michael A. Weinstein

CULTURE CRITIQUE

Fernand Dumont and New Quebec Sociology

Michael A. Weinstein

St. Martin's Press
New York

All rights reserved. For information write:
St. Martin's Press, Inc., 175 Fifth Avenue, New York, NY 10010
Printed in Canada
First published in the United States of America in 1985

ISBN 0-312-17883-2
ISBN 0-312-17884-0 (pbk.)

Library of Congress Cataloging in Publication Data has been applied for

CONTENTS

About the author

Michael A. Weinstein teaches political theory at Purdue University. He is the author of numerous books in contemporary political philosophy and social theory, ranging from *The Wilderness and the City: American Classical Philosophy as a Moral Quest* and *The Polarity of Mexican Thought* to *The Political Experience, Living Sociology* and *The Structure of Human Life: A Vitalist Ontology.*

Introduction

Culture Critique and New Quebec Sociology

"En fait la culture . . . n'est jamais . . . Tout au plus est-elle un projet sans cesse compromis."
Fernand Dumont

"Ne pas se dissoudre surtout, ne pas se dissoudre. Rester, résister, être encore . . ."
Ionesco

Quebec's signal contribution to the sociology of culture is curiously little-known outside this French-speaking, would-be nation in northeastern North America. Perhaps this is above all because in Quebec itself, it is not so much a mere object of knowledge as a lived social project. As such Quebec sociology of culture extends beyond the reflexive hermeneutic circles of intellectual production in the academic disciplines, beyond the government apparatuses' encodings of instituted meaning, and even beyond the subsidized beggardom of Québécois artists (writers, painters, *cinéastes*), to indicate a generalized social praxis. And so a permanent interrogation: how does one live in a language that is not that of the dominant North-American modernity? How does one translate modernity into Québécois when Barthes, for one, defines modern being as knowing what is no longer possible?[1] It is precisely because Quebec culture in this questioning is so inherently sociological that it is worthy of more serious examination, for the Quebec experience is unique: an unravelling within one human generation of a culture at the level of a society as a whole.

Preeminently dialectical, Quebec culture is above all an outstanding work of consciousness that has moved in time from the medievalism of the late '40s to the postmodernity of the present, and in space from a locus that shifts through every paradigm of intellectual discourse. Never exclusively the priviledged articulation of an intellectual clerisy, nor the coded analytic of the legislator, nor the reified passion of the artwork, Quebec culture is simultaneously a permanent debate between all three addressed to a fourth presence (*le peuple, la nation, la société*) in the event of a response. If Fernand Dumont, Quebec's premier philosopher of culture, can write that "In fact culture never is... At best it is a project ceaselessly compromised,"[2] this is because Dumont's are not the last words, only the first, for, ceaselessly compromised, Quebec's eminently philosophical culture always returns to its question.

For 20 years, in every facet of social life, Quebec practised what was termed *rattrapage* or catching up, absorbing in two decades traditions that France and the United States had evolved over centuries. The resulting tension (which is most apparent in the new sociology of thinkers like Dumont, Marcel Rioux and Guy Rocher) proved to be more, however, than a profound internalization and reconciliation of French methodology with American structuralism, but the *dépassement* of both in a distinguished *synthèse* which gives Quebec thought its characteristic stature. For always there would be, against the elaboration of systems originating from either the university or the development policies of the state "*pensée-État*"[3], the *critique* provided by Quebec artists, whose signifying practices constitute an unremitting global refusal of the sufficiencies of

Science and Power. In the constant movement from *critique* to *dépassement* to *synthèse*, Quebec's most striking contribution to the sociology of culture, from the attempt to elaborate a unique cultural discourse, has been in uncovering the extent to which discourse is itself uniquely cultural.

CRITIQUE
Culture in the absence of culture

Since the resounding 'No' of the May 1980 referendum — in which the Parti Québécois, elected in 1976, asked for a mandate to begin negotiating secession from the Canadian confederation — Quebec culture has taken on the universally strained features of postmodern trauma. Allan Wallach's critical formulation has become programmatic:

> Cut off from the one possible source of an alternative historical vision, the avant-garde only managed to keep alive a bohemian culture of opposition. And even this culture of opposition could not long outlive its own commercial success. Today there are no authentic avant-gardes, only moments of opposition staged by politically aware individuals.[4]

From spiked hair to the return of basic black, it's Quebec's *grande noirceur* or the '50s again plus electronics. After a 20-year explosion of *parole*, Quebec culture has succumbed to lifestyle's pluralistic organization of uniformized post-historical daily existence. With the dissolution of the independentist body-politic that collectively embodied Quebec's first self-conscious culture, there is left only the physical culture of the atomized body: culture inscribed in the flesh. As Pierre Vadeboncoeur writes in *Trois Essais sur l'Insignifiance,* culture that "once again must be fled."

> In 20 years Quebecers have depleted the
> principal of their culture: beliefs, *mores,* rites,
> imaginary, ancestral preferences; overturned
> their social organization, family, school,
> parish, petty wage-earners' economy; (and)
> repudiated their traditional teachers, their
> secular advisers.[5]

An awesome silence has descended. "But this silence all of a sudden," writes Normand de Bellefeuille.[6] "Only the eyes are still capable of uttering a scream"; with this line from René Char, Léa Pool opens her 1984 feature film *La femme de l'hôtel.* Mutism, alienation, indifference, suicide and failure haunt recent Quebec cinema, in features such as Jean Beaudin's *Mario* (1984), in Pool's *La femme de l'hôtel,* in Denys Arcand's *Le confort et l'indifférence* (1982), in Jean-Claude Labrecque's *Les années de rêves* (1984). And in *La dame en couleurs,* Claude Jutra's first French-language film after nine years of self-imposed exile in English Canada, it is the triumph of institutionalized culture rooted in private anguish and madness. Disenchantment and *inquiétude* penetrate poetry and the literary journals:

> Endemic depression that has abutted onto a
> sort of amnesia, an apparent indifference, a
> false unconcern thinly covering repressed
> stupor, invisible culpability and unnameable
> rage, as though all has been disenchanted and
> falsified.[7]

Quebec today, writes Laurent-Michel Vacher, is "in a state of shock following the triumph/defeat."[8] But what has triumphed and what has been defeated?

Since 1948, with the publication of the Quebec surrealist manifesto *Refus global,* it has been here, as Marcel Rioux has argued, "that the most important ruptures in the social imaginary have manifested themselves."[9] According to the suicide-poet Claude Gauvreau, *Refus global* "With a sense of prophecy unparalleled in the twentieth century . . . realized that all attempts at revolution . . . would be doomed to failure unless they made a clean break with all the mental habits inherent in the logical evolution of Christian civilization."[10] Which was to say, 30 years before the fact, that culture in Quebec would be postmodern or not be at all. In the prophetic words of *Refus global*, "The society born of faith shall perish by the weapon of reason . . . "[11] The achievement of Quebec's modernity, then, would be the work of the "weapon of reason," and its "universal law," its "positive philosophy of action" (as Pierre E. Trudeau wrote in 1950); that is to say, the instrument of the state. And its locus would be in the attempted conjunction of consciousness and culture (as Fernand Dumont wrote in 1958).[12] At the heart of this ambivalent dialectic of state/power and culture/intellectuals was a question, as Dumont was perhaps the first to recognize: "What sort of self-consciousness, of seizing of consciousness (*prise de conscience*), would permit the 'man from here' (*l'homme d'ici*) the culture termed French-Canadian ?"[13]

A traditional answer was provided by the state in 1961 at the beginning of the Quiet Revolution, with the creation of the Ministry of Cultural Affairs, first of its kind in North America. The new ministry, in the words of Quebec's then-premier Jean Lesage, "will be so to speak a ministry of French-Canadian civilization . . . the first, the greatest and the most efficient servant of the French fact in America; that is to say, of the soul of our people."[14] Far from being a break with the mental habits inherent in the logical evolution of Christian civilization, the cultural project of the Quebec state would embody its continuation, stemming from religious thought and the Roman Catholic institutional heritage, but tinged with the modern *will to efficiency.*[15] As such, it offered to provide in secular form a stabilizing counterpoint to the surrounding dynamic modernity that Henri Bourassa once called "this immense sea of Saxonizing Americanism."[16] Yet 20 years later, the Quebec government 1978 White Paper on cultural development would admit that the secular state had scarcely improved on the traditions of *la survivance* in decrying the present-day state "of advanced deculturation in which we find ourselves."[17] In a highly nuanced assessment of the modern institutionalization of culture in Quebec, Carolle Simard notes that "By means of cultural development, one of the principal axes of the rise of Quebec society, the state gave itself the means to exercise its tutelage."[18] The Quebec cultural institution would not only represent the retreat of social autonomy before the inroads of politics but as well would serve as a locus for the uniformization of social practices, which within the cultural institution itself would translate into the rise of professionals and the specialization of tasks.

In the view of Montreal newspaper *Le Devoir* cultural editor Robert Lévesque, the officially instituted culture managed by a cadre of cultural bureaucrats would amount to little more than "a marginal affair." After 24 years, the Ministry of Cultural Affairs and cultural development policy were still "perpetuating the moral torment of artists reduced to begging year after year."[19] For Lévesque, however, the foresaking of the macro-culture to the "reality of the lived" stemmed from the Parti Québécois' refusal of the cultural and political break with the past in the promise of which it had come to power. As a result, Quebec official culture thus would shift from an original cultural *action* founded in a language to the elaboration of cultural *policy* considered as an instrument of development. The shift would be accompanied by the rise of a professional order for whom, both within the cultural institution as without it, specialization would go hand-in-hand with the reinforcement of relations of authority and domination. "In reality," writes Simard, "we are ... passing from culture (considered) as a tool to culture as an agent of social control."[20]

Few Quebec intellectuals have been as pitilessly lucid in their grasp of this fatal passage implicit in Quebec's cultural project as Fernand Dumont.

> If power has largely contributed, as has the development of knowledge, to breaking the ancient collective structures of values, it also attempts to impose new ones: but it is here that it must inexorably fail. From where, in fact, does it derive its proper legitimization? Behind the slogans about private initiative, behind the policies that aim to provoke the consent of employees to the norms and ideologies of enterprise, one can see only particular interests and one cannot perceive through what transmutations they would turn into values unanimously recognized as being those of the collectivity. These powers come to have no other justification but those they fabricate for themselves: and that is the fatal consequence of the process by which they substitute themselves for culture in order to tend towards the exercise of the monopoly of culture and signification.[21]

Few would admit, as Dumont does, that the modern intellectual's use of the political power of the state to give birth to a new society has been "an enormous act of failure (*acte manqué*)", understood in the dual sense of an act that failed and an act that failed to take place. Or fewer would suggest, as Dumont does, that in the critique of culture, it is the cultural critic himself who stands on trial, having to defend "the profound sickness" of contemporary culture in its relations to the world. With supreme rigor Dumont describes man's tragic aspiration towards a transcendent *avènement* and equally tragic entrapment in the empiricism of *événement* in the tripartite dialectic of the failed vanities of art, science and organization's investiture of contemporary culture. For, undermined by organization, culture re-emerges "as a sub-product of organization; it can no longer descend upon existence as an *avènement...*".[22] Deprived of culture's given by organization, it is for Dumont nevertheless upon the atomized, denuded individual "that rests the immense and impossible task of giving himself at the same time a culture and a society." Yet that individual, as Dumont recognizes, has been penetrated by organization "in the most direct manner now, in the very essence of private life."[23]

In the absence of culture, Dumontian man is "condemned" to *"produce"* or "fabricate" one through "the variants of technical action . . .: to give itself a history, consciousness must *believe* in a history that does not depend on itself alone."[24] To Dumont's 1958 question ("What sort of self-consciousness . . . would permit the 'man from here' the culture termed French-Canadian?"), two possibilities can be advanced (in keeping with Dumontian dualisms such as *avènement/événement, distance/mémoire,* etc.): nihilism/fideism.

But, as early as 1948, *Refus global* had given notice both that these were dead-ends and the two sides of the same fatal dialectic: "The society born of faith shall perish by the weapon of reason." For *Refus global*, and in particular Paul-Emile Borduas, there was still a third possibility for culture in Quebec.

DÉPASSEMENT

The artist as prophet

> Borduas from 1949 onwards must be seen firmly in the perspective of *dépassement,* of movement beyond, a perspective which was to become 20 years later, and after his death, that of a large part of Quebec society.
>
> Marcel Rioux, *artscanada*

There is no more searing and prophetic vision of Quebec's fate in the modern century than the artistic productions of Paul-Emile Borduas. Borduas' work has, of course, a double moment of significance: both as political biography and as prophecy. As political biography, Borduas was the fantastically courageous and creative force behind the writing of that famous manifesto of artistic resistance, the *Refus global*, which with its call "to make way for magic" and for the emancipation of the poetic imagination marked just that frontier of resistance in the Quebec mind where the clerisy and the ruling bosses were put on warning that their dead power had reached its limits and that a new Quebec was on the upsurge: a "collectivity of the future."

> *To hell with incense-burners and holy-wine-sippers! They exhort a thousand times over anything they have ever conferred. Reaching over their heads we are able to touch the ardour of human fraternity to which Christianity has become a closed door. The reign of this hydra of fear is ended . . .*
>
> *From the reign of repressive fear we pass to the reign of anguish. One would have to be made of stone to remain indifferent to the pain ever-present behind the masks of forced gaiety, behind the psychological reflexes which induce inhumanly cruel excesses (who can fail to weep with horror at the news of that horrible collection of lampshades made from the tatooed skins of unfortunate prisoners on the orders of an elegant lady; or cry out at each endless recitation of the torments suffered in the concentration camps; or be chilled to the bone at the description of the dungeons of Franco's Spain, of indefensible reprisals and cold-blooded revenges?) This reign of all-powerful anguish brings the reign of nausea in its wake.*
>
> *The fatal regression in morality from a collective force to one that is strictly personal and sentimental has*

woven an extra lining for the already double-sided screen thrown up by abstract knowledge, behind which society skulks to devour in ease the fruits of its betrayals. The last two wars were necessary for an appreciation of this fantastic state of affairs. The horrors of the third world war will solve the impasse once and for all. Already the rats of Europe are trying frantically to build an escape bridge across the Atlantic.

Meanwhile our duty is simple: to break finally with all the conventional patterns of society, to oppose openly its opportunistic spirit. Refusal to exist below the level of our psychic and physical possibilities. Refusal to close our eyes to the crimes of society, to the confidence tricks perpetuated under the guise of wisdom, of "services rendered", of "return for due favours." Refusal to be billetted in the one village of plastic arts: a well-fortified post but one that can too easily be outflanked. Refusal to be silent — do with us what you will, but hear us you must — refusal of glory, of honours: the stigma of all that is injurious, unconscious, servile. Refusal to obey, to be made use of for such ends. Refusal of all INTENTIONS, the evil weapon of REASON. Down with them both, down to second place!

MAKE WAY FOR MAGIC! MAKE WAY FOR OBJECTIVE HAZARD!

MAKE WAY FOR LOVE!

MAKE WAY FOR NECESSITIES!

Liberty can come only after the most violent excesses of exploitation. They will constitute these excesses. They are fated to assume this role, and no particular "leader" will be necessary to assure it. The feast will be lavish. We have refused our share in advance.

This then is our "culpable abstention." So make your carefully organized rush for the spoils, clustered around the festering heart of a decaying society ! For us, unpredictable emotion ! For us, the absolute risk of total refusal !

We prefer to be spontaneous, unmalicious cynics.
               (excerpts from *Refus Global* [25], 1948)

For the bourgeois nationalists of the Quiet Revolution — those who made a "carefully organized rush for the spoils, clustered around the festering heart of a decaying society" — Borduas has always been viewed as having a blood-entitlement to being one of the precursors of that profound change in the Quebec mentality which resulted finally in the death of classicism in Quebec, and in the victory of the liberal technocracy of the 1960s. Borduas' political legacy. The "spontaneous, unmalicious cynic" was absorbed by the *parvenus* of the Quiet Revolution as their elegant tombstone.

Paul-Émile Borduas, *Expansion rayonnante*

But over and beyond the "magic" and "objective hazard" of the *refus global,* Borduas has another, darker moment of prophetic significance. He is the artist who tells us the how, why and what of nihilism as the flip-side of Catholicism, and who warns us that Quebec must either be creative in the postmodern condition or perish. Taking "the absolute risk of total refusal," Borduas was one of those rare, capacious minds who exercized the terrible temptation to stare straight into the abyss of existing. Indeed, it was after Borduas had fled Quebec and was living in exile in the Paris of the 1950s that he began a series of paintings which are an eerie and ominous prophetic vision of the darkness within the Quebec of the 1980s. If Borduas' artistic imagination can be viewed as an early warning system, first for Quebec's rupture with Catholicism and then for Quebec's absorption into the modern project, Quebec's fate now is the unhappy one of disappearing into its own black hole. That, at least, was the diagnosis and conclusion of all of Borduas' last paintings.

Only an artist who had lived through in bitterness the last temptation of Catholicism and who understood with a terrible lucidity that the breakdown of the Catholic mind issues in only a "desert of the Will" (Camus) could have painted *Expansion rayonnante.* Etienne Gilson always said that the Catholic mind was fully modern just because it ran alongside and parallel to the central cultural discoveries of the modern period. If this is so, then Borduas understood at once that the disintegration of the Catholic mind as the locus of Quebec society was the "cataclysmic event" which had ushered in the dark dream of the gnawing rats. *Expansion rayonnante* is as grisly and brilliant a meditation as can be found on Quebec's rupture with Catholicism and its ejection into the nihilism of the modern project. In an excellent, and otherwise insightful article, "The Death of Signs: Borduas' Last Paintings", Francois-Marc Gagnon says of this work:

> An early black-and-white painting, evokes
> some cataclysmic event at the origin of space
> like the "big Bang" of modern cosmologies.
> But the matter in expansion is some form of
> galactic dust – or "black hole" – gaining on the
> white space, aiming to absorb the whole gra-
> vitational field into nothingness and transfer
> illusory space into opaque matter.[26]

Borduas was never more *the* Quebec painter than in the unrelenting sadness of his visual reflections on the death of society. The "cataclysmic event": the sudden disappearance of Catholicism as the locus of Quebec identity; the "matter in expansion": Quebec society in the modern project; the "black hole": all signify Quebec disappearing into its own black hole as it substitutes *le virage technologique* for the dream of the New Jerusalem of the North. "The death of signs" is the "decaying society" of Quebec itself as rupture and transgression against the technological dynamo. This is not to intimate, of course, that Borduas at any point attempted a direct translation of his poetic meditation on Quebec in the New World into his visual art. But it is to say that Borduas *was* capable of creating the night-marish vision of *Expansion rayonnante* because his struggle with and against the Quebec legacy took him to the outer limits of finally understanding the nihilism of the "will to will" as the disappearing centre of postmod-ernism.[27] In meditating upon the "Quebec way", with its fateful movement from medievalism to postmodern-ism, Borduas was catapulted into the role of a prophet at the height of his times. After all, only a thinker who has moved, and deeply so, through the formal recitative of Catholicism (the religion of the *dead sign*) could immediately grasp the rhetorical, topological, and for-mal qualities of postmodernism. Borduas' "total refusal" of Catholicism and, with it, the refusal of the master signifiers of INTENTION and REASON (*le refus global*) made him the painter *par excellence* of society as dead, vacant space, and of technology as deprival.

Paul-Emile Borduas, *Composition 43*

But if *Expansion rayonnante* speaks of the contemporary century, and with it Quebec tracing a great implosion towards disintegration, decay, and cancellation, this is just a brilliant opening onto the mood which is set in all of his last paintings. Indeed, if Heidegger is correct in noting that "mood" is the essential truth today, then the mood conveyed by Borduas' artistic imagination is anguish as the key existential tone; black as the dominant colour; the exterminism of the sign as the major thematic; the upsurge of the darkness within as the predominant visual metaphor; the privileging of space over time as the purely rhetorical epistemology of postmodernism; pure instrumentalism without signification as the dynamo; and the visual depiction of a world that is *only* a matter of topological space, of pure figuration without meaning, and an almost crystalline sense of existence as deprival.

Paul-Émile Borduas, *Composition 69*

In much the same way that Susan Sontag has written of Artaud that he was the artist of an indescribable and almost unbearable pain within, an artist who wrote in and through the language of pain, Borduas is the artist of "obstinate torment."[28] Indeed what is most captivating about Borduas' work is that there is no break between the steeling of his grisly insights into postmodernism during his exile in Paris and the physical decomposition of his artistic productions. When Borduas paints in the language of nihilism, he gives the wasteland a tongue. Even the actual physical produc-

tion of his artistic work traces a great path of disintegration and decomposition. As François-Marc Gagnon
notes, the last paintings are not titled. They are
presented for what they actually are, "literal significations":[29] Composition 43, Composition 69, as if in
gazing into the "abyss of existing", Borduas also refused
any *trompe-l'oeil* that would distract the eye from the
death of the sign. That, at least, is one lesson of Composition 69 where the overpowering presence of the
dark dream is *not* interrupted, but rather enhanced, by
the light colouring at the top. There's no edge at all in
this painting, nor even "tension" in the modernist
sense. The "white" in the painting is much like the
lightning-flash which, as Foucault has said in "Preface
to Transgression", illuminates the dark immensity of
the sky for an instant, then disappears as the rupture
which confirms the reality of the night.[30] The "white" is
the cut that enhances and finally verifies the nebulous
density of the black dream. And, of course, there can be
no more vivid a vision of disintegration than Borduas'
last "Gitanes" paintings. What's most noteworthy
about these last drawings (completed on the liners of
Gitanes cigarette packages) is the fact that there is such
a close parallelism between the physical production of
the art and the visual metaphor which it works to
provoke.

> It is well-known that towards the end of his
> life, feeling too weak to work on the big
> canvasses, Borduas got into the habit of long
> stays in bed where he wrote, painted a little
> and mused on his Parisian bad luck. One day
> he got the idea of ripping apart the ubiquitous
> Gitanes cigarette packages which littered his
> place, and on the liners of these he painted, or
> drew, a series of 21 small and unforgettable
> works in India ink, using a brush and some
> times a pen. Jean-Paul Filion, who visited his
> studio immediately after his death, recalled

Paul-Émile Borduas, *The "Gitanes" Paintings*

having seen his bedside table cluttered with "ink bottles, pens and brushes".[31]

Borduas gives us art and existence as *rubble.* In his book *Closing Time,* Norman O. Brown perfectly caught the spirit of the times when he said this would be a century that privileges decline and, in fact, marks decline as the aesthetics of seduction itself. The "Gitanes" series is brilliantly seductive: all of the drawings are struck in the style of hyper-decline and hyper-decay. Here, as Gagnon notes, not even a "minimum of dichotomy" is maintained and with "its disappearance, the signs were erased."[32] But Gagnon is not entirely correct: there is *one* sign left which is the emotional mood which unifies what is otherwise the bleak and despairing erasure of depth and the privileging of a purely topological space through the whole Gitanes series. And that sign is *sadness* itself as the emotional combinatorial of Borduas, Quebec's "spontaneous and unmalicious cynic."

SYNTHÈSE
New Quebec Sociology

Utopia and fatalism are the main psychological poles of the Quebec mind. This is one culture which is decidedly *not* static and, for that reason, lives out the tension (in video, dance, literature, politics, and theatre) between the antinomies of political resignation and social utopia. The tension of living in a world on the edge and the colouration of public debate and private sensibility by intense and shifting "moods" make Quebec such an innovative forum for new cultural possibilities in North America.

Indeed, Quebec may be *American* in its technology and *French* in its historical and intellectual lineage, but it's definitely *latin* in the sheer emotional intensity and brinksmanship of its politics and culture. Quebec is one society where Weber's Protestant Ethic has met its match in a popular will to preserve the *vouloir-vivre*

(Aquin) of daily (non-market) culture, and where there remains a very real space of political contestation, from the militancy of public-sector unions to the "culture groups" that spring up everywhere. In the television culture of North America, Quebec is a social anomaly. It's a *real society*. Here culture can be a lived social project horizoned by a constant media debate on the meaning of the "Quebec fact" in the New World. Living in Quebec is being part of a society, almost a family, that is contentious, politically combative, and crackles with intellectual energy. And New Quebec Sociology is its truth-sayer, almost the barometer of the "family feud" which is Quebec today.

While the Quebec artistic imagination moves to the fatalistic, whether in the final paintings of Borduas or in the unrelentingly grim writings of the novelist Hubert Aquin (a nationalist of the blood kind who, with the political victory of the Parti Quebecois in the 1970s, saw the handwriting on the wall and put a gun to his head*), the opposite reflex of the Quebec mind is represented in all its brilliance and desperate energy by the tradition of New Quebec Sociology. Borduas paints the triumph of an empty, signifying culture and the death of society, but in the Quebec sociological imagination it is the reverse that takes hold. Resolutely utopian, it affirms the vitality of the social and check-mates the postmodernist vision of the world on its down-side with a realistic, often up-beat, vision of an emancipatory society. In Quebec sociology, social movements rise and fall; media theory is played out against the actual background of a society being blasted apart by American television; the cityscape is studied with an active and haunting sense of remembrance of how recently and massively this society was propelled from an agricultural to an urban idiom; and questions of alienation, powerlessness, and ideology-critique are posed in the grander terms of a philosphy of culture.

* "I am the fractured symbol of the Quebec revolution, but also its disordered reflection and its suicidal incarnation," *Prochain Episode,* 1965

Quebec sociology is *not* just a professional idiom: it is an active, public record-in-the-making of Quebec' struggle to become a main site for an emancipatory culture and technology in the midst of the entirely bleak landscape of postmodernism.

What makes Quebec cultural sociology so brilliant, and, in fact, an entirely original innovation in twentieth-century sociology, is that it represents a dynamic synthesis of the most *avant-garde* tendencies in French *and* American sociology. Quebec sociology is French and American sociology in new key and, perhaps, in new intellectual expression. Like Quebec society which traces its historical ancestry to France, but whose very economic and cultural survival depends on understanding the technological dynamo of the United States, Quebec sociology may be influenced, and even tempered, by key tendencies in French social thought. Jean Baudrillard, Jean-François Lyotard, Edgar Morin, Pierre Bourdieu, Alain Touraine — these French thinkers do define a large part of the Quebec intellectual milieu. But Quebec sociology's most critical edge consists of a deep and extensive dialogue with American social thought. The famous tradition of Quebec community studies and ideology analysis bears the mark of the pioneering work done in Quebec in the early part of this century by the American sociologist, Everett Hughes. Marcel Rioux might begin his writing career with a study of *Île-Verte* and Fernand Dumont might reflect on the absent culture of *St-Jérôme*, but Hughes was the precursor of this rich tradition of ideology analysis and community studies with his classic account of the sociology of Drummondville.[33] Quebec urban sociology with its highly original studies of the cityscape is the critical sociology and pragmatic naturalism of the Chicago School of the 1930s, from Dewey to Mead and Parker, still alive and well in the Quebec of the 1980s. And the bitter debate in American sociology between Parsons and Mills or what's the same, between technological liberalism and cultural Marxism, is reproduced in Quebec sociology as a critique by the best and brightest of Quebec sociologists of the hyper-functionalism of the Quebec state.[34]

Quebec then, is, the main intellectual site in the New World for the reception of French social thought into the North American context, and for testing the main theses of American sociology — liberal or Marxist — against the reality of contemporary Quebec society. Quebec sociology is the *lieu* where the *formalist* bias in so much of French thought (from the social morphology of Durkheim, Mauss and Gurvitch and the hyper-structuralism of Deleuze, Derrida and Kristevà to the dead semiology of Lyotard, Baudrillard and even Pierre Bourdieu) meets the *pragmatic naturalism* of American social thought. Quebec sociology ignites to produce a brilliant flash-point between Durkheim's *"conscience collectif"* and Parsons' "institutionalized liberalism" on the one hand, and, on the other, what remains as a theory of society when Alain Touraine's analysis of social movements as the upsurge of real history encounters the "information society" of Daniel Bell.

From this double absorption has emerged a highly original, eloquent and comprehensive tradition of Quebec sociology — New Quebec Sociology. The Quebec sociologist, Guy Rocher, puts it best:

> One of the advantages of Quebec is that it situates us at the confluence of work in the English and French languages. It is necessary to take advantage of this situation, since these two languages suffice for the moment to keep us in touch with the principal currents in sociological research.[35]

What Rocher does not say though is that Quebec sociology has done much more than merely keep "in touch" with key tendencies in American and French sociology. It has actually *transformed* the tradition of contemporary sociology, and this by forcing the very best and most critical tendencies in French and American sociology into a new synthesis. English-Canada may have produced many of North America's leading communication scholars and theorists, from the liberal visions of Marshall McLuhan, Northrop Frye and Eric Havelock to the critical perspectives of Harold Innis and George Grant.[36] Contemporary American thought might privilege visions of technicisme *par excellence*, from the technocratic populism of Alvin Toffler — that electronic Elmer Gantry of the 1980s —to the technological determinism of B.F. Skinner, Buckminster Fuller and Daniel Bell. But the Quebec mind *excels* in cultural sociology. *Culture critique* in the form of synthetic interpretations of "total society" is the key word of Quebec sociology in the modern century.

But because so little of Quebec cultural sociology has been translated into English, it has never enjoyed the critical attention in North American discourse it so richly deserves. This screening-off of the major contributions of Quebec sociology is all the more a profound loss since, in the twentieth-century, Quebec sociology has experienced something of a golden age that has resulted in highly original and compelling studies of technological society, and in the creation of *alternative* social visions. French thought today might be caught up in the sump-hole of poststructuralism, and American thought might be turning pragmatic to the hyper, but only Quebec cultural sociology is in a genuine *ascendancy*. It is the physics of political resistance against the dark dream of postmodernism.

Thus Guy Rocher (who, along with Marcel Rioux and Fernand Dumont, is one of Quebec's *key* cultural sociologists) may have studied under Parsons in the 1950s but he returned to Quebec to write a remarkable three-volume introduction to a "general sociology".[37] Indeed, Rocher's "general sociology" represents nothing less than an entirely original synthesis of major tendencies in French and American sociology as viewed through the *lens* of Quebec. Even the titles of the different volumes of Rocher's general sociology are misleading (1. *l'action sociale;* 2. *l'organisation sociale*; and 3. *le changement social*) to the extent that they provide no indication at all of the rupture with conventional sociology which this work anticipates, but which is, curiously enough, signalled by the subtitle of all three volumes: *Regards sur la réalité sociale.* For what Rocher is after is the critical reconstitution and transformation of the sociological tradition itself. Refusing the *pragmatic subordination* of so much of American sociology and the *productivist subordination* of orthodox Marxian analysis, Rocher's sociological imagination seeks simultaneously to comprehend the logic and dynamics of *actual* social reality (technocratic society), and then to find a way by which Quebec might move beyond the poles of tradition and technocracy. Rocher writes, therefore, a critical sociology which is at the height of its times: a sociology which is *historical* in its sensibility (Rocher describes sociology as both a reflex of history and as a "*science-en-situation*");[38] which gives primacy to the question of *culture* (for Rocher, culture means the space of a "lived social project"); which is at the frontiers of the discursive analysis of *ideology* (the third volume of this work is an almost classic study of the ideology of technocracy and revolutionary movements); which is sensitive to the immersion of the "self" in the massive *organizations* of contemporary existence (it's "adaptation" as a potentially suppressive *or* creative force);[39] and which strikingly puts "*society*" back into sociology (Rocher writes often of the "historicity" of sociology).

All of which is to say is that Rocher is the "Comte" of Quebec sociology, and this in a double sense. *First,* rejecting cultural relativism on the one hand and an "ahistorical" sociology on the other, he seeks out a new grounding in praxis and analysis for a "scientific sociology." Rocher's scientific sociology is, however, critical and dualistic. It's *critical* because it walks the edge where sociology "as immersed in its object of study, society itself"[40] begins to "distance" itself as an

intellectual reflection on the social milieu; and it's
dualistic because it seeks to mediate the deep tensions of
contemporary society: organizational inertia and social
movements; cultural emancipation and economic
determinism; tradition and technological society.
Rocher's *sociologie-en-situation* is thus in the order of a
grand, synthetic effort at mediating the antinomies of
contemporary society. *Economically,* it refuses the
double subordinations of "class" and "interest-group",
and turns instead to an analysis of actual social movements, their ideological discourses and the social formations which represent their historical context. *Politically,* Rocher's *sociologie-en-situation* is neither sectarian
(he is, after all, the author of a "general sociology")
nor a technological liberalism (he plays Durkheim and
Mauss against Parsons) but a study of culture as an
actual social project. *Socially,* Rocher's vision privileges
neither "traditional" solidarities (Durkheim's organic
solidarities) nor the "mechanical" solidarities of technological society, but valorizes instead the need to
"create" a social identity at the borderline of need
(immersion) and desire (dispersion). And *aesthetically,*
Rocher's general sociology is dualistic because, in
refusing all social monisms and in resisting the empty
temptation of a pluralistic universe, it insists on the fact
that sociology is, in the end, an "ethical project": a
great and continuing effort at synthesizing the estranged
poles of twentieth-century experience.

There is a *second* way that Rocher is a latter-day
Comte. One of Comte's central preoccupations was the
deep fissure in modern experience which had appeared
with the eclipse of military (*theological*) society and the
upsurge of *industrial* society. Rocher can take to Comte
so well ("Comte is, above all, the student of modern
organization")[41] because Comte's major inquiry — the
gap between traditional and technological society — is
also the real predicament at the base of Rocher's general sociology: a *sociologie-en-situation* that operates at the
boundary of Quebec's rupture with medievalism

(Comte's "theological" society) and postmodernism. Like Comte, Rocher's thought is at the borderline of the disintegration of traditional society (Quebec's Catholic and rural past) and the emergence of telematic society (the United States as Quebec's future). If Rocher's general sociology can be so fresh, persuasive and urgent and, in fact, represents such a powerful synthesis of classical European sociology and contemporary American social thought, this is because it both *names* the central political (and existential) problem of Quebec in the twentieth-century — the shattering of organic solidarities under the pressure of *le virage technologique* — and, moreover, seeks to respond to *la crise* by providing a new ethic: a critical and interpretative sociology which, if it does not succeed in healing the wound opened up by the "modernization" process, at least makes of the act of synthesis itself (holding the "antinomies" of modern experience in a dynamic and harmonious balance) the beginnings of a new, and entirely postmodern, Quebec sensibility.[42] Rocher's is thus a "general sociology" of the most rigorous order: it walks the borderline between cultural relativism and technological universalism. And if Rocher's sociological imagination can reorder the whole skyline of classical and contemporary social theory (from Durkheim, Toennies, Weber and Marx to Parsons, Mills, Mumford and Malinowski) this is because it contains a larger project that is the real text of all of his writings. And that project is nothing less than a desperate act of synthesizing the classical (European) origins of sociology with contemporary (American) theories of technological society as a way of illuminating the dark horizon which *is* Quebec today on its own borderline between a double abolition: its disappearance as the *cité de la liberté* on the northeastern frontier of the Americas, and its absorption into the consumer frenzy of the technological dynamo.

Rocher's treatise in "general sociology" is decisive to the extent that it *marks* the real social tension in

Quebec today. It nominates the almost unbearable tension of a whole society forced to exist *dualistically* — between tradition and technocracy — just as it provides the jumping-off point for the culture critiques of Rioux and Dumont.

Thus Marcel Rioux — Quebec's leading *critical* sociologist — can be the Sartre of the New World because all of his writings, from his earliest ethnographic analyses exploring the popular culture of *Ile Verte* in the St. Lawrence River and *Belle Anse* to his master text, *Essai de sociologie critique,* combine a critical exploration of Quebec popular culture with a superb, almost layered, analysis of key cultural transformations associated with the consumer society of advanced capitalism. Rioux can write so eloquently about the "primacy of culture" because of his main claim that culture itself is today the strategic terrain on which is played out the decisive struggle between emancipatory social movements and the forces of ideological hegemony. Moreover, Rioux can even go so far as to make "a sense of moral indignation"[43] one of the ground categories of critical sociology since all of his intellectual and political activity over a thirty-year period from editing *Possibles,* a review of Quebec popular culture, and writing over ten key sociological texts to satirizing the liberal, and federalist, turn of Pierre Elliott Trudeau has concentrated upon a single, major theme: cultural sociology as the *critique* of the existent institutions of late-capitalist society; and as the *creation* of a new, transformative vision for Quebec in the twentieth-century. For Rioux, Quebec is a "laboratory" of new ideas and new politics in North America because it's in Quebec that the fall-out from the hyper-pragmatism and militant war-spirit of the United States clashes head-on with the irresistible will to survive of the Quebec *peuple.* For Rioux, the *survivance* of Quebec society and culture means that if Quebec in the 1980s is not to be, as in the old Catholic dream, a "New Jerusalem" of the North — a Catholic and French nation swimming in the sea of Protestant and English North America — then the survival of Quebec culture might be that of a small, independent, French, and socialist society. In a word, a real *alternative* to telematic society. The critical sociology of Marcel Rioux embodies that delicate transition-point in the Quebec mind where the now-*passé* Catholic vision of Quebec as a New Jerusalem is transformed into the secular, but equally prophetic, image of Quebec as the New Albion. As Rioux puts it in the conclusion of his *Essai de sociologie critique*:

> If one carefully examines what has gone on in Quebec in recent years, it does clearly seem that it is here that the most important ruptures in the social imaginary manifest themselves. In relation to the United States and France, Quebec presents a particular case, a sort of hybrid of time and space. A people of space, like Americans, (but) a people that nonetheless experienced, because of the defeat of 1760 (and) the failed rebellions of the 19th century, a historical trauma which propelled it backwards towards time past. To justify its existence vis-a-vis the dominator and its right to survival, a great number of definers of (Quebec's) situation had to invoke history and the past, adopting an attitude of withdrawal and suspicion with respect to the future that marked the first rupture with their Americaneity; that is to say, with the fact they had always turned towards space and the future. And that they had proved by crisscrossing the entire continent and leaving their mark just about everywhere: limited to Quebec, they (nevertheless) continued to open up the territory and ceaselessly make it into a new land. This mixture of time and space in its social imaginary gives the Québécois the particular character that distinguishes them at the same time from Europeans and Americans.[44]

Rioux's Quebec is the tension between *time* (France as the past) and *space* (the future of the United States) in the New World or, what's the same, between Empire and Civilization as Quebec struggles between the possibility of *popular culture* (rooted in a dialectic of remembrance and creation) and the *power* of technological society.

However, if Rioux is a socialist, populist, satirist, and agnostic on the question of popular culture, then the opposite, deeply religious, side of the Quebec philosophy of culture is represented most brilliantly by the sociology of Fernand Dumont. *Heideggerian* in his seminal insight that culture is both "memory and distance," *Christian* in his aspiration for the revival of the religious sense in contemporary life, *anthropological* in his study of the domain of cultural significations and practices, and *liberal* (of the progressivist kind) in his politics, it is in the writings of Fernand Dumont that Quebec culture fully becomes a tragic *philosophy*.

Torn between nothingness and credence, man is an uncertainty. But, unlike animals, he can *locate* that uncertainty in language. Language thus becomes referential — it produces names — at the same time, however, as it interrogates. Language, Dumont would say, is the "stylisation" of man's "incessant *inquiétude*." It is the expression of man simultaneously as his search for himself *and* as his work. Language is at once criticism *and* establishment. As criticism, it is the text of man's distanciation; as establishment, it is man's record that he has been/is/could be. Language is the *sign* (as Dumont speaks of the "wound" of consciousness, one could possibly speak of *stigmata*) of man's *dédoublement*, and consciousness is its "mystery." As the awareness of his own *dédoublement* both from the world and himself, man articulates a second, doubly reflexive language and with this rupture produces the fatality of cultures.[45]

"Inasmuch as it is forbidden to grasp the absolute origin of language it is not possible to reach the ultimate founding of culture,"[46] yet Dumont distinguishes between *culture première* and *culture seconde. Culture première* is a given, the facts of a signifying universe of the social disorganization of human *parole. Culture seconde* could be defined as the values of a signified universe of the social organization of language. The relations between primary and secondary culture are ones of "conversion," of rupture and *déchirement*: of distance and its regrets, of consciousness whose unease stems from its ability to remember the *culture première*.[47] But, remembering, *culture seconde* is also the understanding and explicitation of *culture première*: "Epistemology achieves itself and thus transcends itself in the elaboration of a culture."[48] *Culture seconde* or, more precisely, its *dédoublement, culture savante* (lit., culture that knows) is thus to *culture première* what theology is to religion, law to custom and jurisprudence, science to technique (and the social sciences to social techniques).[49] In a word, what cultural theory is to culture: its achievement and transcendence to an autonomous, self-reflexive *référence* "that constitutes itself only by the production of (cultural) works."[50] *Culture savante* is the "agnostic field"[51] in which to test the mythological significations of (popular) cultural practices against the nihilistic hardness of scientific experimentation with "the double chimera of realism, the subject in itself and the object in itself."[52] The social (or textual) productions of *culture savante*, in the infinite displacement of reference, are, however, "less the product of the social division of labour than the product of a division of cultural labour,"[53] a division of culture in which the *intelligentsia* participates and which it attributes to itself in its uneasy displacement from the common culture. For Dumont, the theoretization of *culture savante* calls fatally for its *dédoublement* in a sociology of the intellectual (which has yet to be written.)[54]

CRITIQUE/CONCLUSION
THE QUESTION OF DUMONT

If new Quebec sociology has been a distinguished contribution towards a full sociology of intellectualization, one should be able to — provisionally at least — make an attempt at assessing its development. To do that involves a return to the question first raised by Dumont in 1958: What sort of *seizing* of self-consciousness would permit the man from here the culture termed French-Canadian? In other words, the question raised by Dumont — the question of Dumont — must be an interrogation of the Quiet Revolution itself, that Quebec-wide classroom for an intellectual generation's institution in modernity. Thus, was it an authentic school, an original school, or was it just the same old *duplessiste* catechism, but in a business suit now instead of a *soutane?* This was Dumont's own assessment in the early '70s:

> At a moment when a little people of nothing at all that spoke badly . . . was interrogating itself as never before as to this idiom . . . (t)here were . . . those who taught the French language here or who allowed their children to learn it, (but) who asked themselves whether or not they were succumbing to some archaism condemned by history, (who asked themselves whether or not) they were unduly perpetuating obstacles that would prevent the next generation from *finally joining the life and mechanisms of American civilization* . . . .
>
> A people which had never invented anything the least bit official: (not) democracy, (nor) literature, (nor) capitalism, (nor) development. A people from nowhere. Without category or status in diplomacy or in systems. Reflecting upon it, it was a privileged situation.[55]

The Quiet Revolution, then, was the attempt to overcome *that*, to become a "laboratory," "an experimental society:"[56] "Quebec — and this is one of its rare privileges — thus recapitulated in a very short time the inherent dialectic of the development of the West."[57] But what if, as Dumont also suggests, this experimentation, the creation of new, original values was also the re-creation by modern means of displaced traditional values?[58] The written invention (the conjunction of technique and knowledge) of an original corpus of secular social thought and an original class of official secular thinkers — of which Dumont is the outstanding example — also had its *dédoublement* in the social constitution of a modern (technocratic) business-class. But the highly educated graduates of the Ecole des Hautes Études Commerciales (Quebec's Harvard Business School) were destined not, like the official Quebec intelligentsia, for the public sector with its ideology of the *collective* good; 95% of the HEC's 1984 graduates would be absorbed by capitalist, *private* enterprise.[59] For that realization, too, is the achievement of the Quiet Revolution's "experimental society". but now as the nihilistic experiment of the technological postmodern with its commodity lifestyle — a culture *in the absence of* culture. Yet still within the slender hope of the Québécois language's claim to be that which is no longer possible.

Trapped between (technological) nihilism on the one hand and (linguistic) faith on the other, Dumont's question remains, like the hanged man at the end of Huxley's *Brave New World*, turning, turning, turning, but never able to rest.

So it can perhaps be said of Dumont, in Renan's words, what Dumont himself said in the epigraph of *La Vigile du Québec*:

> Let us remember that sadness alone gives rise to great things, and that the true means of uplifting our poor country is to show it the abyss in which it is. Let us remember above all that the rights of the *patria* are inalienable and that the little with which it considers our advice does not dispense us from offering it.[60]

Michael Dorland/Arthur Kroker — Montreal

1

Prologue: Rêve Noir

I shall undertake here briefly a personal and appreciative criticism of Fernand Dumont's thought, a recurrence to it from the viewpoint of what I affirm in it and what I must deny. I affirm those aspects of any thinker that evince existential insight, deep conversance with the richness and texture of life experience seized from within by the individual. And I reject any symbolic healing of the rents and agonies revealed by existential insight. The task of life-philosophy is, for me, to be as concrete as possible in describing personal existence. The task of life-strategy is to find ways of affirming life in the light of existential insight.

The vein of gold in Dumont's thought is his poetry. I have learned from Fernand Dumont that one of the dispositions that I must take towards the world, in order to live in existential truth, is an obstinate torment. The essence of obstinate torment is that the flesh is divided and refractory: desires war with one another and the most intimate desires are never satisfied. The dream of April, if realized at all, is transient; the mood of September perdures. The real void in our existence is the gap between desire and satisfaction; a perfect emptiness, spaceless and irritating because of its vacancy. We do not get a proper response from things at the most primal level, yet as long as we live we beat against them and each other. We must do so because the extinction of desire is the extinction of life. So long as we affirm life at all we affirm obstinate torment, the repetition of the gap between want and its gratification.

Beyond obstinate torment in the sphere of concrete existence is nothing but terrible patience, the ability to withstand the tormented cries of the world and the suffering, dispersion and hatred that they indicate. This is the ascesis offered by Dumont, the existential discipline to accustom oneself to an existential predicament. If we are to follow the existential Dumont we must persist in obstinate torment in a spirit of terrible patience. I consider this prescription to order the highest kind of virtue of which our century is capable, the complete and concrete appreciation of the forms and contents of finite life. Through keeping the distance between desire and its objects as a permanent structure of awareness one becomes capable of a joy in real and transient consummations that winds itself around torment without abolishing it. This joy seems to be known to Dumont only in flashes, because he looks elsewhere than his own terrible patience to remediate the torment. He tries to heal symbolically.

From an existential viewpoint, outside his poetry, Dumont's thought may be seen as an attempt to overcome his existential insight through sublimation. The primary sublimation, which grounds all of the others, is the founding of his own project in the dialectic of *sens* and *absence.* This is itself a *dédoublement* of the primal frustation of desire in the world. We only come to raise the question of the sense of the whole because we have been horribly frustrated by all of the parts. Or, the search for a sense to the whole is a compensation for a life that has tasted its own failure and knows that the contents of concrete and finite life are inadequate to gaping want. The long cry into a boundless night sounds out the judgment of our failure. The study of the articulations of that cry with the goal of redemption from the agony of the profane is what Pascal called a diversion. *Absence,* when defined in relation to *sens* and not desire, is an abstraction that diverts one in both senses of that word from the matrix of lived experience. It is a place holder in a new matrix made of thought, the *imaginaire.*

Once Dumont has carried out his primary sublimation he uses it as a critical weapon against more attenuated and abstract sublimations. Everything from now on takes place in the *imaginaire.* But, of course, Dumont's power as a social critic comes from the fact that technological society subsists in the *imaginaire,* its roots in the air of abstract thought where they become dispersed, dissipated, and desiccated. From the basis of his primary sublimation Dumont shows that no extant anthropology overcomes the absurd. Indeed, the most advanced anthropologies are the systems of rational postulates of the social sciences which try to cut off from all content and thereby become discarnate. The social sciences are the reflective side of the complex organizations that despoil traditional culture and move towards hegemony over popular culture. Life is becoming void of spontaneous content, sucked dry of vitality by the technosphere. Desire is not what we feel from within, but calculated suggestion. Here Dumont is a profound critic and diagnostician, but he has for a therapeutic only the recovery of a past already spoliated. He counts on the historian to graft a dead root onto the tree of life and to make that root live. The hopelessness of this project is tempered for Dumont personally by his Christian faith, but it stands out starkly in his quest for utopia.

As a public philosopher Dumont is hounded by the consequences of his own social criticism. He dreams of a *cité de la liberté,* democratic, socialist, and nationalist (an update of nineteenth-century liberal nationalism), but he cannot give it a ground. If he looks to the present he finds only the intentionality towards the *événément* of predatory technocracy, the society of operations. But if he looks to the past he finds it only in reflective memory and not as prolonged into lived *durée.* Hence, he becomes utopian in a pejorative sense, calling upon the interpreters of the *culture savante* to restore somehow a living link with the contents of life, which are enclotted in an inert tradition. He wishes for a spontaneous popular culture to emerge, but his reading of society pushes him into an elitism and vanguardism which crystallizes in a dream of a young technocracy dedicated to resuscitating tradition as it moves forward into an experimental democracy. The tensions in this vision cannot be reconciled. If anything the new middle class in Quebec is less continuous with the past than were the uprooted liberals of 1837. The members of this class inexorably tend to choose the technological society and its leading imperial and multinational entities just as their forebears chose to compromise with an earlier capitalist imperialism. And the same holds throughout the world, wherever tradition is dead and the society of operations regnant. If revitalization of politics is possible it is only through a more profound affirmation of life born of terrible patience, which is short circuited by Dumont's utopianism.

Dumont's proposals for cultural planning (the void of St.-Jérôme filled by the *culture savante*) and experimental democracy (the resistance of technocrats against technocracy) have been passed by in the wake of 1970. Embattled in a predatory world of economic dislocation, the elites of Quebec return to the historic compromise mapped out by Garneau and prefigured in Dumont's own appeal to vanguardism. They bargain with powers who will not permit a small nation to experiment freely. Dumont's own analysis of the society of operations interprets this situation precisely and his existential insight permits us to see that its essence is the alienation of desire, the abstraction of desire through its seizure in the calculated suggestion of operationalizing thought which produces *ad hoc* traditions to realize immediate organizational goals. To recover desire means to desublimate, to suffer obstinate torment, to cultivate terrible patience, and finally to allow oneself to joy in the divided flesh so that it may be regenerated from within.

2

The September Mood

To understand Fernand Dumont one must cultivate a September mood, the mood evoked by his aptly-named collection of poems, *Parler de Septembre.* For Dumont is most deeply an existentialist and, more particularly, a theistic existentialist who is a proper counterpart to Martin Heidegger. He experiences a stangeness in the world, an estrangement that harbours the craving for a union that will not altogether abolish distinctness. Close to nature, indeed intimate with it in his poetry, Dumont has devoted his life as a thinker to highly generalized and sophisticated studies in the philosophy of social science. He uses the social sciences as paradigms for a global theory of culture that opens out to a philosophy of history, the aim of which is to be thoroughly critical. Here, too, the similarities to Heidegger are evident.

But underneath the brilliant dialectics there is always September to which those dialectics must at last be relative, as both the *esprit de logique* and the *esprit de finesse* had to cede in Pascal to *existenz.* For Dumont September means to suffer an "obstinate torment" as he wanders among things that do not respond to his "strange desire", the "dream of April." There are other seasons, the ecstasy of the summer moment, the despair of unremitting winter, and the joy of spring birth, but it is early autumn or not quite autumn that places all of the others in perspective: life is still present and with it, perhaps, hope yet the signs of death are unmistakeable. There is an uncanny melancholy in September, a wish to enjoy what is left of the season of happiness, though a gnawing acknowledgement that all spontaneous union with nature is finite. This leads at best to a kind of serious happiness, a reflectiveness that mutes ecstasy, and, in its most severe phases, to a sadness that threatens to give way to despair. September, as Paul Tillich might say, is "on the boundary".

> L'arbre toujours pousse sur les mots
> Comme un secret supplémentaire
> Feuilles vainc contrée de la mémoire
> Dont Dieu éparpille la couleur
> La femme dont mon âme est la tige
> Ainsi que la mort y trouve sa demeure
> Toutes deux se souviennent que je veille
> À quelque présage
> De tout ce blanc qui rêve d'avril
> De septembre mon désire étrange
> Haute la nuit sombre ma main
> De quel avenir de quelles semailles[1]

"L'arbre toujours pousse...," *Parler de Septembre*'s introductory poem, can be interpreted on two levels, one strictly naturalistic and the other Christian, a duality that reflects the "obstinate torment" that is Dumont's most profound response to the melancholy mood of

September. The poem is divided into three four-line stanzas, each of which is unified by a dimension of time, past, present, and future, respectively. Memory is the theme of the first stanza, presence of the second, and desire of the third.

The first stanza reads: "The tree always pushes on the words/As an extra secret/Leaves vain country of memory/On which God squanders color." The first two lines provide in striking imagery the dominant mode in which Dumont articulates the resistance of the world to desire. The tree, mute but alive, displaces the words that might have been illusioned enough to believe that they were adequate to Being. For Dumont, "Since men have spoken, since they have written, they have wished to lead the silence of the universe and their intimate savage purposes back to bounded horizons and grounded anguishes. To inhabit the world: This was, perhaps, from the first a long cry into a boundless night, like the cry of someone lost in the woods."[2] Through historical experience the cry becomes more articulate, but the words never map the woods in such a way as to give them intelligible form. The tree, then, displaces man, and, in Dumont's thought on culture, causes man to displace his own language in ever more extravagant feats of abstraction, which themselves beg for mediation. But the tree remains, despite human vanity, the primal, unintelligible, and uncontrollable force of life or, perhaps, even of Being. It contains an extra secret that culture cannot fathom because no rational operation is adequate to it.

The second two lines of the stanza portray the concrete phase of nature that is September. Here there are the perplexities that arise from obstinate torment. The leaves are a vain country of memory, beautiful tokens of a pretension that symbolize September's agony of delight and sadness. Their beauty belies their transiency and, indeed, their death: God has squandered their color on them. And here is another theme close to the core of Dumont's thought: No more than the world can God be fathomed.

In the first two lines of the second stanza, in striking naturalistic imagery, Dumont proclaims the radical estrangement of being-in-the world. The woman, identified with the tree, has the grafted trunk of Dumont's soul, through which death has found an abode. Dumont has written of himself as an explorer of "absence," someone who might write a *"Treatise of the Void."*[3] Here the void is expressed most primally and concretely as the presence of death in the soul and through the soul in life, represented by the tree and the female, the Other. One may find here resonances of Jean-Paul Sartre, but the separation of *pour soi* from *en soi* is far more intimate for Dumont, who entwines them together in a paradoxical dialectic. The second two lines of the stanza comprehend the existential response of Dumont to the agony of September, depicted as the presence of death in life. Both the woman/tree and his soul remember that Dumont is attending to some omen. The Heideggerian tracings are deep here, recalling the task of "listening for Being." The response of attentiveness, of being alert to what might be hidden, expressed only fragmentarily or incompletely in ordinary lived experience, is Dumont's last line of defense before the Absurd. Or, perhaps, for Dumont the Absurd is another one of those delusive words that seem to complete things when all that they really do is to generate more perplexities. It would be the most abstract word of all, papering over alienation by declaring its absoluteness. Dumont is properly attentive in response to the presence of death in life.

While the past is the preserve of a vain memory and the present a place of attentiveness, the future is a domain of expectation. The third stanza begins with winter dreams of April, the month in which nature is reborn and in which Easter is celebrated. The endless whiteness of winter, one of Dumont's key symbols for alienation, gives way in spring to endless variety and growth: April is the counterpart of September, its inverse; the memories of winter are easily forgotten and the prospects of joy seem boundless. But from September Dumont feels a strange desire in the high night that darkens his hand. There is a future and there are seeds of that future, but their meaning is not known. The last stanza summarizes the themes of the first two by placing them in the orientation of futurity. The attentiveness of the present, a *disponibilité* in the sense of Gabriel Marcel, has not been able to decipher the omen, but bears itself towards the world as a strange desire enveloped in a darkness that does not permit any light to be cast on the future. Death is overwhelming, or only seems so, since there is also something like hope, the expectation that is analogous to hope when one's God is beyond the bounds of reason but still offers a promise. Here, indeed, there are resonances of the long and dark night of the spirit (the strange desire) of which the Spanish mystics wrote. At the the end of the night is April, now only a dream, and, it appears, there is stubborn doubt about what it will hold. This perplexed and questioning expectancy grounds a deep humility in Dumont that is personal and also for all men. We are profoundly alienated but we strive to overcome that alienation through our words, which never fit Being completely, but which we are called upon to utilize repeatedly, though in full knowledge of their intrinsic inadequacy. Like Heidegger, Dumont is finally or most fundamentally passive and contemplative towards Being, though the passivity is restless and the contemplation is strained taut and never released into the self-enjoyment of fulfilled meditation. Dumont entitled one of his works *The Vigil of Quebec*. He might best be thought of as the vigilant existentialist, who is attentive to the past, though he knows that it is gone irretrievably; watchful in the present, though he is torn between life and death; and expectant towards the future, though its eventualities are an enigma. The September mood is a difficult one to sustain because it demands such keen awareness of the ambiguity and ambivalence of life as we experience it.

To affirm that mood one must embrace decay in beauty, death in life, the starkness of black and white framing expectation and dream. And, as will be evident later, one must still act to create and sustain goodness in the world, though such action has no more than problematic results. Dumont's vigil, though he would probably demur, is heroic in the existentialist sense, recalling *The Myth of Sisyphus* and *Being and Time*. It is a form of what Karl Mannheim called "Titanism," the life of centering oneself in solitude towards the *mysterium tremendum et fascinans*.

Although the autumnal moment is for Dumont the *durée* that forms his sensibility, leading him to a vigil that gathers up memories of a past reclaimed for life only by present commitment that attends expectantly to a puzzling future, September is not complete. At another pole from autumn is summer, the season in which *existenz* is transfigured into Being, not transcendent Being, but the concreteness and self-sufficiency of the lived moment in which the love of man and woman is fulfilled, though instantaneously. In his poem "Ton visage mes mains..." he writes: "This instant encircles us and we are it."[4] Such an overflowing of any determination that can be given in words is one of the hallmarks of Dumont's mind: even the most profound and comprehensive descriptions leave something out and what is neglected often turns out to be of equal or perhaps even of greater importance than what has been placed in the foreground. Here, in the summer poem, the gnawing sense of time and the impending death of variegated nature are replaced by that other time, the lived present, and, indeed, one that unites, albeit fleetingly, two persons, each of whom, from the standpoint of *existenz*, is radically isolated by the frustration of importunate desires breaking upon the world. The incompletion in his poetry, a lack of resolution raised to the level of pitting the unresolved against the self-sustaining, makes it impossible ever to define Dumont by any characteristic mien. September is primal only because it makes transition so conspicuous, juxtaposes opposites, and defies a sense of completion; but it only evinces those qualities because it does not include those tastes of fulfillment, without which there would be no basis in intimate life for the strange desire, the dream of April. Personal existence is primary in Dumont's thinking, but momentary experience can exceed it, abolishing separation through union.

Dumont's universality makes him seem to be almost a pure cosmopolitan, living, as José Ortega y Gasset put it, "at the height of the times." Yet also in a strictly Orteguian sense, Dumont is close to his circumstances as a Québecois, drawing from Quebec perhaps more than from anything else the inspiration for the substance of his thought. Dumont describes the tension between universalism and particularism, on which is superimposed the agony of standing between the learned culture that he has made his life and the popular culture that constitutes his inheritance, in striking personal imagery. He relates that in his study where he writes are two photographs, one of his father Philippe Dumont, at the side of the turbine on which he worked in a factory in Montmorency; and the other of his master of youth, Gaston Bachelard, who taught him the special being of language and particularly of learning, that to be " 'born in writing, by writing' " is the " 'great ideal of the great solitary evenings.' " Both his father and his master, Dumont reflects, would throw up their hands at the books that surround him, the first in the incomprehension and disbelief of someone who had never written anything, and the second in the exquisite frustration of acknowledging: " ' I study ! I am only the subject of the verb to study...' "[5] Dumont remarks that Philippe Dumont and Gaston Bachelard are "two beings whom I have greatly admired and loved, who have taught me not only some ideas but some images of life, some things that have remained dear to me."[6] It is Philippe Dumont, however, who, representing Quebec, has had the more profound influence than Bachelard,

symbol of the modern world of scientific reflection;
just as the dialectics of the social sciences find their
import, in Fernand Dumont's work, in his obstinate
torment in the world. The legacy of Quebec is the
silence of the repressed, of those who were delegated to
fulfill through their sweat the designs of modern industry. In his poem "Du seuil d'où naissaient nos jeux..."
Dumont, recalling a day when he was coming of age on
which his father took his hand, sings of the silence of
Quebec: "The wind had laden me with the silence of our
fathers/With the violent with the obstinate silence/Of
those who know nothing/But stark bare life/Where the
word so hesitates/That it rouses at last/Only the live
coals of the world."[7] Dumont's most intimate project,
which centers him in the particularities of history, may
be understood as the attempt to give voice to what lies
beneath the violent and obstinate silence of Quebec.
But to make that effort is to lead Quebec beyond itself
into the equivocal world of modernity and, perhaps,
to make it lose itself. And so in trying to give voice,
Dumont must always turn upon his origins, feeling
somewhat at a loss and even deficient, but also concerned to remember the "bare life" out of which the
hesitant word can sometimes rouse the "live coals of
the world."

It is Quebec, one may surmise, that has allowed
Dumont to pursue the remarkable project of combi-
ning the nineteenth and twentieth-century minds without, assuredly, being able to fuse them. His thought
most resembles that of the great turn-of-the-century
philosophers in Latin America, particularly the Mexicans, who appropriated the modern European culture of their time and forged it into a unique expression
of life in their special circumstances thereby adding, of
course, a new contribution: the defense of the contra-
rational against instrumental reason and its concrete
expression, industrial imperialism. The Mexican philosophers, José Vasconcelos and Antonio Caso, expressed the spirit of self-conscious nationality that leavened

the Mexican Revolution of 1910, placing that Revolution in the context of Western cultural and social dynamics.[8] Dumont may be understood as performing a similar role to that of the Mexicans for Quebec's "Quiet Revolution" of 1960, which coming a half-century later than the others in the New World bespeaks how heavily the yoke of imperialism weighed on the Province, though its imposition might have been less violent than elsewhere, and how persistently the Québécois tried to cling to a past inexorably dissipated. Dumont, in Arnold Toynbee's terms, is neither a Herodian, who supports the order of rationalized empire, nor a zealot, who clings to an eroding tradition, but a man on the boundary who searches the past for the threads of continuity that might be woven into an alien and measureless present so that a more meaning-filled future might be possible. Again it is useful to recall Pascal, who, by turns, was cosmopolitan and provincial, scientist and humanist, and most profoundly existential and Christian. Living in an earlier phase of modernity, Pascal centered himself in philosophy of religion, whereas Dumont finds his axis in philosophy of history; but both of them share a sensitivity to what is despoiled by scientific rationality simultaneously with an appreciation for the power of reason to transform life while seeming to transcend it. Seen as a philosopher of Quebec, Dumont is illumined as a profound and brilliant expositor of the agonies of modernization, not clinician or patient, but, in Nietzsche's sense, an experimental being who comprehends both.

In his *Le Lieu de l'Homme,* a work that seeks to "discern the nature of present culture and to glimpse the drama that torments it," Dumont claims that his perspective is "very general and at bottom simple."[9] One might suspect Socratic irony here, but there is truth to Dumont's assertion that his thought avoids complications and intricate involvements in detail. At least the root of that thought evinces an elegant simplicity to which further refinements are added, as a tree spreads its branches and covers itself with leaves. Simplicity and generality also make Dumont's thinking eminently accessible, despite its immense range and density of learning, because all of the special investigations, replete with demarcations of their limits, can be led back to the root. There is an essential connection between the starting point of Dumont's intellectual endeavors and the September mood of obstinate torment which feels the foreboding of an unresponsive nature. In Dumont as philosopher one encounters the most proximate influences of German phenomenology and existentialism, particularly the thought of Martin Heidegger. Dumont's poetry and philosophy fall along the lines marked out by Heidegger when he declared that "the poet names the holy" and that the philosopher is the "guardian of Being." In his poem "Puisque l'espérance se boit à lentes gorgées..." Dumont gives his version of the poet's task: "It is necessary for the word to begin/To gather up the course of the days/The unripened songs/The fleeting warmth of the hand/The hasty anger/The light steam that leaves injustice at the world's doorstep."[10] Yet the word must also fail to achieve its purpose and here Dumont does not allow poetry to escape from the incompletion of human existence. He writes in "Profond dédain et infinie couleur...": "Words are lost thoughts/At the side of God who rests/At some tree at some care."[11] It is not only the language of poetry that incarnates "lost thoughts," but all languages. Yet the word must also begin to "gather up the course of the days." The necessity and the failure of speech, and then of all the variants of language, is the simple and general thought that sustains all the rest of Dumont's reflections.

The agony of the word appears in Dumont's most comprehensive meditations as the struggle of man to give sense to himself through placing himself intelligibly in the world, a struggle which is ceaseless and ever frustrated. In "Puisque l'espérance..." he writes: "There will have to be much time and snow/For the word to tremble and divine/Heaven's fire or God's shadow/Blind to metaphors."[12] That striving of the word to "tremble and divine" Being or even its tracings is thematized philosophically in all of Dumont's prose, but most clearly in his masterwork *L'Anthropologie en l'Absence de l'Homme,* where he presents his most concise statement of the human condition. In his attempt to provide a definition of man, Dumont, though he recurs explicitly to Aristotle, is much closer to the Heidegger of *Being and Time:* "If one wished to propose a first definition of man in a few words, one could admit this one: a hypothetical being whose principal concern is... to define himself."[13] For Dumont, as for the early Heidegger, there can be no direct communion with Being; it is necessary for man to inquire into himself because his own problematicity, here his "hypothetical" being, disturbs any easy belief that the final truth of things is given to him by the world that surrounds him. Human beings are, then, in Maurice Merleau-Ponty's terms "condemned to meaning." Dumont, in a "free paraphrase of Aristotle" suggests: "... man is an animal who speaks, who utters his existence rather than describing it, and a political animal, who imagines his world with others rather than inscribing himself in a milieu."[14] To utter existence is primally the "long cry into a boundless night" that Dumont evoked in *Le lieu de l'Homme.* There he wrote that "to inhabit the world has been also, without doubt, the slow recovery of the articulations of this cry and of the shores that it strained to reach."[15] Dumont's intellectual project may be understood as a continuing and a heightening of that task of recovery, which is undertaken in the lives of all human beings, but which, when raised to critical reflection, becomes the organizing theme of all thought.

Dumont compares the primal cry to that of someone "lost in the woods." Here his existentialism takes on a specifically Canadian tone, echoed in George Grant's *Time as History:* "Our present is like being lost in the wilderness, when every pine and rock and bay appears to us as both known and unknown, and therefore as uncertain pointers on the way back to human habitation."[16] For Dumont, as for Grant, man seeks to make of the wilderness a home through the creation of culture, the intention of which is to be "a dwelling where nature, our relations with the other, the weighty traditions of history would be confronted with conscious intentions in a never-completed dialogue."[17] To emit the first cry is to initiate history, which carries with it always, through all the phases of its procession, both the appeal to a response from the Other and the constitution of a substitute for that response, because that response is never granted unequivocally and satisfactorily. Beneath culture, then, is frustration and, perhaps, the eerie terror of radical uncertainty and isolation so deep that culture can never entirely heal it. Yet culture is man's destiny and vocation, because man must fall back upon himself and find in the successive articulations of his cry the habitation that nature has denied him, not merely because his essence is out of joint with those of other things, but because his own being is hypothetical and, therefore, incomplete.

If there is one term in which Dumont's thought can be readily encapsulated, it is "*sens.*" In *Les Idéologies* he presents a ground for ideology that can also stand for other forms of culture: "Individuals and groups act in order to resolve the uncertainties of the situations in which they find themselves. ... To confer a sense (*sens*) to the situation by action, to recognize a sense (*sens*) to the situation so that action is possible: it is initially in this elementary conjunction that ideology takes root."[18] The term "*sens*" is best understood, as Dumont uses it, in the rich and wide-ranging set of meanings that it has in the French language, including sensation, feeling, judgment, intelligence, meaning, interpretation (indeed, all of the manifold operations of the mind and their products), and perhaps, most importantly, way and direction. To confer *sens* is to attempt to find one's way out of the woods, to transform the primal cry into a verbal map of a habitable world. It is clear, then, that *sens* should not be confused with the English word "meaning," which normally connotes a bias towards intellection and, indeed, abstraction, and which may sometimes create the illusion that "meanings" are strictly separate from the things to which they refer. However abstract the articulations of the cry become as culture specializes, they arise from attempts to confer *sens* in the most concrete way: "The most trivial of my conducts, before being engaged in knowing the world, modify my standing in it."[19] And that standing (*emplacement*) is always already saturated with *sens*: "What we call sometimes 'real life' is only conceivable through our imagined lives. Existence is, on the whole, only the ashes of our representations."[20]

If man begins his history as a hypothetical being who, lost in the woods, craves that the wilderness be a fit habitation for him, he is, for all his efforts to confer *sens,* in Dumont's view, never sucessful in constructing for himself a home. The counterpoint to *sens* in Dumont's thought is the void (*le vide*). Dumont, the theorist and creator of culture, the defender of speech against silence, is also the philosopher of "absence." Immediately following his definition of man as an animal who utters his existence, he writes in *L'Anthropologie* that there is "... consciousness because there subsists in us an opening, an absence that our conducts explore without filling it."[21] That absence, though, is fertile, subsisting as the multitude of counterparts to the different ways in which *sens* is conferred. The long cry into a boundless night, winter's desolation, is the reciprocal of the fulfilled present of summer and the dream of April. In the section of *Parler de Septembre* entitled "Seule La Neige", Dumont writes in "La terre partage avec le ciel...": "The earth shares with the sky/ The slow torment of confidence/All the dreams crack."[22] There are scissions, cracks, fissures, gaps, and vacancies throughout human existence. The boundless night is itself a void, but the cry creates a new displacement, a *décalage*, an unwedging of utterance and the rest of Being, including man himself, since existence is "only the ashes of our representations." And as man turns upon himself to inquire into his being and to define himself, new absences open up. Modern thought about man is anthropology in his own absence, because to give himself standing man must account for himself through his circumstances, thereby losing sight of himself in his endeavours at self-transcendence. And even more deeply, as a hypothetical being, man never finds himself in his self-examination, because that inquest is always conducted within the *imaginaire*, the domain of what he might possibly be that nonetheless is still an approximation of what he is; indeed, in one sense, is all that he is. *Sens* and *absence* are the master terms of Dumont's thinking, nowhere summarized more cogently than in *Le Lieu de l'Homme:* "Culture is, for man, distance from himself to himself. It is, simultaneously, the origin and the object of the word."[23]

The interrelation of *sens* and *absence* in the constitution of culture can be grasped through a third term that is central to Dumont's philosophical vocabulary: *dédoublement,* that is, division into doublets. Culture, as the attempt of man to complete, resolve, or fill (*combler*) the great absences that run through his existence is not merely a supplement to a world already given in its essential features, but that needs some additions to fulfill it: a doubling of the world, a second world neither entirely separate from primary nature nor altogether adequate to it. Indeed, one should not even speak strictly of primary nature, because man is so enveloped in the culture he has created that nature itself comes near to being a product of interpretation, one of the domains of the *imaginaire.* At times Dumont seems even to draw near to idealism, as when he states that what is called "real life" is only conceivable through our imagined lives, or when he substitutes an "epistemology of pertinence" for the traditional concern of the theory of knowledge with truth. Gagnon, whose comments on

Dumont's work push his thought in the direction of idealism or, perhaps, towards a cultural realism that would come close to being the same thing, remarks that "if the sciences of man do not truly have an object, the problem of their truth (adequacy of knowledge to its object) becomes secondary for epistemological reflection."[25] But though it is correct to claim that Dumont does not adhere to a copy theory of truth, it is not the case that he operates merely on the plane of culture, seeking to "explain the intentions at the origin of anthropological practices and to extricate their *foundations,* that is to say the cultural conditions of their possible advent and the collective bases of their legitimacy."[26] The sciences of man do, for Dumont, have an object: man himself taken through his involvement in his situation. But that object is continually being redefined by successive efforts to know it, and that redefinition is not only theoretical, it is fundamentally practical. Man is not culture, not a figment of language, but culture is a doubling of the world that intends to emplace man in-the-world more securely, yet that always also displaces him and drives him to new efforts at definition. The claim that the sciences of man "do not truly have an object" can easily arise from attention to Dumont's reflections on all of the successive efforts at redefinition that man undertakes because no given culture succeeds in filling the void. Each fresh attempt at emplacement is initiated from a situation already culturally saturated and so must appear as another sort of *dédoublement*, a doubling of culture itself. But the various doublings of culture do not take place in a vacuum: they are all led back to the first doubling, which is grounded existentially in being-in-the-world. Were Dumont an idealist or a cultural realist it would be impossible to account, first, for why man must confer *sens* on the world, and, second, for why each instance of conferring *sens* is a failure. Put another way, the need of man to confer *sens* is a truth that is adequate to him, though it points to his inadequacy both to himself and to the world.

The *dédoublement,* the interplay of *sens* and *absence,* forms the basis of the dialectical process through which, for Dumont, history proceeds. Dumont's dialectics never achieve a synthesis of *sens* and *absence,* but rather make man's initial tormented predicament even more acute by creating new absences, those between each cultural form. Such gaps are both horizontal and vertical, in the first case between the multitude of specialized cultural practices that have proliferated especially in the modern world, and in the second between "popular culture" and "*la culture savante,*" the pursuits of the many elites that tend to close in upon themselves in hermetic worlds of symbols. The spirit of Dumont's dialectics is captured in his essay "La Sociologie comme Critique de la Littérature" where he compares the poet and the sociologist through an appeal to contrasting variants of phenomenology. He observes that "literature is a phenomenology of the possible, whereas sociology wishes to be a phenomenology of the necessary." However, both the poet and the sociologist prowl around one another's domains, because it is the whole man, man himself and nothing more, who interests them. Their dissatisfaction with the closure of their special worlds is rooted in the human condition: "It is that the situation of man, our common torment, is essentially ambiguous."[27] Indeed, Dumont is clear here that the study of man not only has a formal object, that is, the dialectic of *sens* and *absence,* but even more so, a substantial or material object, our "common torment." Neither poetry nor sociology appeases the torment, though each attempts to do so and even gains some success. Although they lead in different directions both share in the operation of *dédoublement*: "The sociologist and the poet seek to detach themselves from immediate life and from its first expressions. In both cases a *sens* appears little by little and takes on body, a *sens* which is conferred to life as much as it is entrusted to it. And these stages represent successive approximations of an intention of which the work is the pretext before being its occasion."[28] Literature and sociology, having doubled the "first expressions" of culture in different ways, can neither replace one another nor fuse with each other, but they might be able to enter into a reciprocal and fruitful relation. The methods and concepts of science can give literature a more explicit consciousness of its course, whereas literature can provide sociology with "the indispensable criticism of determinism." And here Dumont introduces a variant of what may best be called his dialectic of conciliation, the only kind of resolution he is able to provide for the torment of *absence:* "And, finally, sociology and literature appear to us as the two complementary explorations that will one day perhaps give us what would be, in the widest meaning of the term, an anthropology."[29]

Dumont's discussion of sociology and literature is replicated in all of his studies of specific cultural practices and disciplines. Always one finds the same dialectical pattern of a doubling that abstracts from the immediacy of life and from primary culture, and, through that abstraction, becomes isolated from the totality of existence and then turns back, not only to primary culture, itself fragmented by all of the doublings, but to other cultural forms that have arisen from similar abstraction and that might provide it with supplementation. It would be accurate to say, then, that Dumont has constructed an existential dialectics that combine the quest of nineteenth-century dialectical thought for unity of man and man, and man and world; and the proclivity of twentieth-century thinking for analysis and discrimination. From the root condition of being lost in the world and voicing an appeal for help, man falls back upon himself and doubles the world, creating a culture that remedies some of his deficiencies but does not provide him with a home. Still homeless, he has no other recourse than to keep doubling culture and thereby fragmenting it, finally precipitating the crisis of modernity, the absence (*défaut*) of integration.

There is no way back to a unified primary culture; indeed, such a culture never existed, but there is the possibility of a network of reconciliations among the fragmented products of *dédoublement*. Such reconciliation may be thought of as Dumont's cultural "dream of April," in the September of contemporary life.

3

Cultural Dialectics:
The Society of Operations

The unbroken thread of continuity in Dumont's thought, as it ranges from the most specialized dialectical relations among concepts in the social sciences to the most concrete poetical images, is guaranteed primarily by the constant understanding of the unbalanced condition of human existence. The paradox of the human project of conferring *sens* on the world is that the efforts of man to emplace himself, to gain standing in his situation, are also displacements engendering distance as much as they secure unification. Attempts at reconciliation that lead to more acute separation; divisions that impel fresh trials at composing differences; these are the deep processes out of which the diverse cultural systems through which man seeks to define himself are created. From his own elegant definition of man as an animal who utters his existence and who imagines his world in the company of others, Dumont works to explore the antipodes of culture and then to construct his dialectics. Dumont does not come upon the various universes of modern culture as a naïve observer who accepts at face-value the current interpretations that the various disciplines which study man and try to transform him give of themselves. Those definitions are entertained by Dumont through his grasp of the human situation and, thus, are inserted within the context of a prior interpretation. That is to say, Dumont is a phenomenologist but his investigations are guided by an existential account of *sens* and *absence,* rather than by the will to be presuppositionless. His freedom from dogmatism is based not on an eclectic tolerance of the significations given to his understanding, but on man's hypothetical being. Dumont does not reduce the cultural systems that he studies to a preordained theory of specific human motives, what Georg Simmel called the contents of human life, but places those systems into the over-arching form of the *dédoublement.* Each specific substantial interest pursued by human beings has, for Dumont, its own integrity, and, indeed, he follows the sociological functionalists in allowing for a plurality of such interests; but each of them is accompanied in its pursuit by the never-completed struggle for *emplacement,* the formal or, at least, general element in human existence.

Dumont does not believe that the nineteenth-century project of synthesizing the sciences through a substantive theory of the origin and goal of history is sustainable in the present phase of modernity. Yet he also eschews the familiar contemporary project of merely analyzing the ground rules of the various human studies. Between the pretension of giving man a determinate standing in the world through showing how his works contribute to an unfolding temporal design, and the humility of letting the expositors of particular cultural practices speak for themselves, Dumont inserts the dual intention of making explicit and precise the multiple interpretations of each discipline, and of providing the constructive addition of orienting those interpretations to one another in the broader framework of dialectics. He thereby avoids being simply a registrar of chaos or an arbitrary speculator. The procedure of leading the diverse products of culture back to their ground in the attempt to confer *sens* and forward to the possibility of bringing them into mutual dependence on each other opens up, for Dumont, the field that defines his major inquiries: anthropology. *Anthropologie,* in Dumont's lexicon, is the most comprehensive designation that can be given to the study of man's essays at self-definition. It includes not only, for its object, the various systems through which man scrutinizes himself and his relations to the world contemplatively, but also, and even more fundamentally, the reflective activities through which he seeks to emplace himself collectively in his situation. Dumont writes in his most systematic work, *L'Anthropologie en l'Absence de l'Homme:* "Anthropology is considered here in a highly extended meaning. It comprehends the sciences of man, philosophy (according to one of its principal dimensions, at least), and even ideologies, since these are properly collective practices of interpretation."[1] Much of the power of Dumont's theory of culture is gained from the generality of his definition of anthropology, the inclusion in it of every knowing pursuit from myth to human engineering, each one brought into connection with the others according to the idea of self-interpretation. The unity of anthropology is diversified most architectonically by Dumont through a dialectical pattern. That dialectic is rooted in the double requirement of giving *sens*: man must confer meaning to his situation through action and must also recognize a meaning in the situation so that action is possible. There is no point for the study of anthropology to begin outside the hermeneutical circle: human existence is thoroughly infected by interpretation, and any analysis and tentative synthesis of anthropologies is based on sets of pre-existent, if conflicting, meanings.

Although in a historical sense human thought has been first and primarily devoted to emplacing man in the world by generating systems of directives to guide the conduct of human beings towards one another and towards their deities, Dumont reverses the genetic order that moves from action to contemplation in his systematization of contemporary anthropology. Modernity in general has, for Dumont, tended towards an imperialism of rational knowledge that involves the relegation of the conducts that constitute everyday life to data that are made available for rearrangement according to specialized postulational systems, the most obvious one of these being the classical economics of marginalism. Thus, it is a basic characteristic of the most distinctive contemporary anthropologies, the human sciences, that they must be integrated with the fuller human life from which they arose. That project of integration is the intention of Dumont's anthropology of anthropologies, which moves dialectically from the "anthropology of operations," through the "anthropology of action," to the "anthropology of interpretation." The anthropology of operations, which is definitive of the human sciences, is the project of vacating human existence of its constitutive and intimate spontaneity, and analyzing it according to sequences of antecedents and consequents that are based on simplified assumptions about human motivation (for example, economic rationality and the related assumption in psychological behaviorism of operant conditioning). For Dumont, none of the human sciences is self-sufficient, first because each one has arisen as an intelligible response to a prior social situation marked by uncertainty and the conflict between unsatisfied demands, and, second because each one has abstracted only a fragment of human intention which must then be related to the others by dialectical analysis. For Dumont, the "reduction" made by the anthropology of operations is "fecund," but "for the anthropologist, for the man that he studies, for the culture that they inhabit, there is an enormous *remainder* after this reduction has been made."[2]

The anthropology of action and the anthropology of interpretation form the dialectical moments in which the recovery of the remainder left by the anthropology of operations is made and its integration with the knowledge gained by the social sciences is effected. Anthropology, for Dumont, is always a mediation intended to emplace man by conferring *sens*, and such is even the case for the anthropology of operations, which responds to the diversification of the modern world into quasi-rationalized environments such as the factory, the school, and the courts. But none of the postulational systems of the social sciences informs life with meaning directly. Knowledge must be taken up by human beings in the conduct of their daily lives and coordinated with those aspects of their situations that fall outside its range. Hence, the second moment of the dialectic is the anthropology of action, which comprehends the cultural practices through which man adapts his theoretical knowledge to his total situation, including prior sets of meanings, diverse and clashing interests, and novel events. Action here is informed conduct, undertaken by human subjects constituting their common life through cooperation and conflict; it is a mediation between the partial meanings yielded by theoretical inquiry and the much fuller and, therefore, complex requirements of concrete circumstances. The anthropology of action does not, as does the anthropology of operations, "suppose that anthropology is, by essence, knowledge." Rather, it is intrinsically normative and is regulated by the "utopia" of the *cité de la liberté* in which human beings freely constitute their common life in concert with one another.[3] Yet even the anthropology of action is an insufficient mediation, because human beings must acknowledge *sens* in their situation in order to confer *sens* to it. Both the rejection of the *sens* given by singular subjects and by collective ideologies that is required by the anthropology of operations, and the fragmentary and immediate nature of institutional practices, "excite paradoxically, as a counterpart, the representation of another world, that of *sens*, as resistant as the one that I collide with when I invoke the presence of nature."[4] The final moment of the dialectic of anthropologies, then, is the anthropology of interpretation, which is based on the fact that social life is always interpreted life: "Society interprets itself, this activity constitutes it in its being as much as do technology or power. Without this activity there would not be, besides, either technology or power."[5] The anthropology of interpretation, when practiced self-consciously, leads to the integration of the prior moments of conferring *sens* by recuperating a totality of meaning through the ever-renewed efforts of a community of interpreters. It is fair to say that Dumont has practiced the anthropology of interpretation in an era of operationalism and functional activity.

The dialectical movement of Dumont's reflection on contemporary anthropology, which proceeds from operation, through action, to interpretation, flows from his understanding of the crisis of modernity. For Dumont, that crisis is cultural and is primarily a product of what Max Weber called "the rationalization of the world." Recalling the principle that in order to confer *sens* on a situation through action human beings must already have acknowledged *sens* in it, one would expect the moments of the dialectic of making *sens* to run from interpretation, through action, and, perhaps, to operation, the latter being an abstract and specialized movement of thought refining the complexities of various activities. That Dumont's dialectic proceeds in reverse indicates the distinctive attenuation of the *dédoublement* in modern times. Modern man, in Dumont's view, has been Cartesian, delimiting sectors of his world for systematization in both theory and action, and thereby creating for himself the illusion that he has been liberated as a free subjectivity. During the course of the modern age the scission that Descartes opened up between subject and object, the former spontaneous and self-dependent, and the latter mechanistic and amenable to rational inquiry, has become progressively more acute as the object itself has collapsed into dis-unity through the proliferation of specialized disciplines. The rationalization of the world has come near to destroying the cultural unity that was characteristic of pre-modern society and has not substituted any new integrative design for it. Thus, the context for human life today is the "society of operations," in which individuals fit themselves into prearranged patterns that are directed towards the fulfillment of circum-scribed functions and never find a satisfactory definition of themselves in their conjoint activities. Sociologically, the division between subject and object is expressed as the split between public and private life, the latter of which increasingly falls under the merchandising and mobilization schemes of the former. Intellectually, that division appears as the confrontation between such modes of thought as behaviorism, which attempt (though never successfully) to eliminate subjectivity, and the existential philosophies, which seek transcen-dence of the self from the position of vacant subject-ivity. Dumont's dialectic begins with the anthropology of operations because contemporary society is operational: mechanism has triumphed over subjecti-vity and *sens* can no longer be acknowledged but must be recuperated and self-consciously created.

Dumont's dialectic of anthropologies is grounded in a philosophy of history based on the elemental struggle of man to emplace himself in the world through conferring *sens* on it. Philosophy, for Dumont, is one of many anthropologies that coexist in the contemporary world, but it is paradigmatic for the others because it so clearly reveals their foundations. Philosophical practice, as Dumont defines it, aims at critiquing "the reification of references": "To insist that these references are only horizons, to institutionalize the critique of them – such is its radical intention. The practice of philosophy, because it is so badly secured, recalls for all the other practices a root that the sciences disguise more or less adroitly under the cover of methods and theories, under the alibi of knowledge." Contemporary philosophy is particularly fit to confute "the alibi of knowledge" because it is the end-product of a series of displacements through which the sciences became autonomous disciplines. Expelled from the field it had delimited and cleared, philosophy "saw itself constrained to take up again in new situations the critique of the relations that man had acquired with the world and to formulate hypothetical designs of the totality that it then proposed as tasks."[6] Philosophy is both the challenge and reformulation of the "total relation of man with his world." It "aims at a *totality,* but one which is neither a synthesis nor an object."[7] Here it is evident why philosophy is particularly revelatory of the structure of anthropologies. The philosopher must "interrogate the *sens* of the human condition in the context of the disarticulation of practice and of culture," and must do so without recourse to any standardized method or procedure that takes objectivity for granted. In reducing the domains of the sciences to horizons that might then be related to one another in a provisional whole, a utopia, the philosopher draws all the other anthropologists into his ken: each also aspires to a utopia, but having dissolved utopia into postulation, is only a philosopher by halves. It is from philosophy that the contemporary crisis begins to be ameliorated.

Dumont's philosophy of history is the aspect of his work that most recalls nineteenth-century thought, particularly that of the classical sociologists such as Ferdinand Tönnies and Emile Durkheim. Following in the classical tradition, Dumont presents a theory of modernization based on the polar types of "traditional society" and "technological society," and, like his predecessors, though even more so, he is disquieted by the disintegration of modern life. Dumont's typology, though substantively falling within the lines marked out by Tönnies's "community" and "society," and Durkheim's forms of "mechanical" and "organic" solidarity, departs from those of his predecessors because it is based on what might best be called a phenomenology of culture. Traditional society is given coherence by an intentionality towards the *avènement* or advent; that is, values and signs are apprehended by the members of the society as being "situated in a sphere anterior to the universe, as if the society was drawn from a dream which was pre-existent to it."[8] Although the statuses and roles of the members of antique societies "evidently had an empirical import," since they "defined modes of work and types of relations and authority," they "constantly gave the impression of being drawn towards the heavens, of having their true consistency in an ideal world."[9] Most importantly, those roles and statuses were, in traditional society, "distributed according to collective values which the society deemed not to have formed itself." In traditional society, then, human beings lived the illusion that the *imaginaire* was a self-subsistent reality, that *sens* was not conferred upon the world by human thought and action, but that it was given to the world and as a world. Dumont has averred that his idea of traditional society, particularly his use of the Greek polis to exemplify it, is a utopia. Indeed, Dumont's discussion might lead one to believe that traditional man was a Platonist and, perhaps, in the most significant respects he was one.[10] Nevertheless, a type should not be confused with an empirical description: it is a standard for the organization of descriptions and, in this case, it points to the condition in which man believes that *sens* is conferred on his life, precisely the belief that can no longer be upheld in the contemporary world.

At the other pole from traditional society is technological society, defined by an intentionality towards the *événement,* or event, that is, "the management of nature and of the human milieu as though society gave to itself its own end."[11] Modernity, for Dumont, is encapsulated in the term "technology," because it is technology that best evinces the project of modern man to found his life on the use of his own reason. Traditional man used techniques, and even judged their efficacy, but surrounded his usages with symbols and values that he referred to the anterior universe and, therefore, he did not reflect on their possible relations to other techniques and, more importantly, to new aims. The modern liberation of reason from shared values and symbols has allowed human beings to posit their own goals and to devise ever more refined means of achieving them. The consequence of technology's permanent revolution has not only been a vast increase in the power of some human beings, particularly the bourgeoisie in the West, to effect their ends, but a loss of *sens* to the world. Instrumental rationality, for Dumont, has broken up the world into specialized environments in which some men fulfill the designs of others and none grasp a totality of meaning. As the modern age has proceeded, more and more aspects of life have been brought under the sway of the *événement*, first through the growth of industry, and then through the attempts of elites to put *sens* back into the world, if only to be able to secure labor discipline, markets for their products, and support for and compliance with their political strategies. In the technological societies of today there is, in many cases, a complete inversion of the intentionality towards the *avènement*: the residue of the values and symbols of traditional society is used pragmatically in functional designs to influence men to comply with the requirements of those designs. Advertising and propaganda become the replacements for myth in the society of operations. But they are not a satisfactory substitute, because they represent the efforts of the part to speak in its own interest for the whole. Dumont's philosophy of history, then, is thoroughly critical in the sense that it comprehensively critiques "the reification of references." Traditional society is not a golden age, but a projection of man's own constitutive powers into a second world: *sens* is acknowledged, not conferred. Modern society is not the era of progress, but a field for the "disarticulation of practice and of culture": there is no *sens* to acknowledge, only proliferating and continually thwarted efforts to confer it.

Dumont's philosophy of history, though it is thoroughly contemporary in its treatment of language and culture, and in its questioning of a progressive unity to historical development, poses problems that are associated with the classical nineteenth-century theories of modernization. In his preface to Dumont's major specialized study in the philosophy of social science, *La Dialectique de l'Objet Économique,* Lucien Goldmann raises some of the major issues concerning philosophy of history in relation to Dumont's thought and thereby provides a context for placing that thought within traditional debates. Goldmann first considers the problem of historical causation, arguing that although Dumont is "perfectly conscious of the strict relation between the historical transformations of socio-economic life and the development of theoretical thought," he "nevertheless overestimates the weight of scientific thought, notably of economic thought, and of the collective consciousness as engines of historical evolution."[12] In Goldmann's view, Dumont especially accords too small a role to "the passage from the liberal economy to the economy of trusts and monopolies, and most of all to the later development of planning." Here the issue of whether or not Dumont is a sophisticated idealist surfaces again. Appealing to the existential ground of Dumont's thought in being-in-the-world, one may respond to Goldmann that the attention in Dumont's work to the most refined products of the *dédoublement* is more a matter of methodology than an indication of a substantive theory of causation. It is not that scientific thought or thought in general is the motive force of history, but that all human praxis is accompanied by the struggle to find *sens* in and to confer it to the world. What *sens* is made of the world in particular historical periods is a function of the kind of life men share, and that life is already saturated with *sens*: it is impossible to disentangle "socio-economic life" from the *imaginaire*. It is, indeed, Dumont's intention to use the theories and methods of the social sciences as indices of other social transformations, such as the rise of complex organizations, to which they are responses. His is a critique of reification that questions the independence of the social sciences from the rest of social life and leads those specialized disciplines back to their functions for social groups and for the global society. Although he insists upon the primacy of the activities, such as work and politics, that emplace man directly in the world, he does not separate *sens* from structure: he is not a structuralist, either in the sense of according an independent meaning to impersonal structures or in that of freeing them from all meaning and analyzing them according to mechanistic dynamics. The motive force of history for Dumont is the struggle for *sens*, which is pursued at every level of life and in each of its activities. Not thought, but existence, grounds history.

A second issue raised by Goldmann concerns the absence of a clearly defined historical subject in Dumont's thought that could serve as the bearer of his participative utopia: "Fernand Dumont never asks which social groups, collective subject, and, to speak clearly, social classes develop and affirm these new values; or which ones oppose them in attempting either to conserve the structures of the past or to establish their privileges in nascent structures."[13] Here Goldmann touches on a more profound bias in Dumont's thought than was the case in his preceding criticism of overemphasis on the causality of thought. Although Dumont recognizes those aspects of social dynamics that embrace domination, conflict, and the quest for privilege, he follows in the line of the systematic sociologists of the late nineteenth century in according primacy to integration, consensus, and solidarity. That he does not believe contemporary societies are integrated, that they can support a coherent world of *sens*, leads him to seek paths towards conciliation rather than to take the road of class struggle. Here Dumont follows such diverse thinkers as Tönnies, Durkheim, and, particularly, Max Scheler and Karl Mannheim, all of whom approached the resolution of the crisis of modernity through efforts to devise ways of peacefully conciliating conflicts, primarily through new modes of knowing (the therapeutics of the sociology of knowledge). Dumont does provide for a collective subject in his thought, but it is "man," not any particular group of human beings who are specially situated to be the instigators of a future society. He is, in his politics, most of all an adherent of that characteristic tendency in French thought, pluralistic socialism, the great nineteenth-century expositor of which was Proudhon and which in the twentieth century has been expressed with greatest lucidity by Georges Gurvitch. Pluralistic socialism has been the unexercised option of modern political thought and, perhaps, that indicates its limitation.

Economics is, for Dumont, the central discipline of the modern social sciences because it emphasizes more than any other the intentionality towards the *événement*. In *La Dialectique de l'Objet Économique* Dumont shows how economics began by liberating calculative reason from any normative constraints and then successively had to try to recuperate what it had ignored in its initial *dédoublement.* In comparison with the other social sciences, such as psychology and sociology, which must "ceaselessly reconstruct schematisations of human actions before being able to apply to them the logic of experimental models and calculation," economics "identifies the angle according to which calculation is no longer conceived of as the manipulation of schematisations that would be pre-existent to it, but as an original intention of conduct."[14] Economics, then, evinces clearly the intention behind the society of operations: the individual is to be freed to exercise his reason in the pursuit of the goals that he engenders. Dumont, of course, does not believe that any but a few individuals actually were so freed or that bourgeois society approximated the principles of marginalism, but uses classical economics as an index of the direction of modern social dynamics and of its tendencies towards disarticulation. The outcome of the liberation of calculative reason has been, indeed, the technological society, which, far from being a realm of individual freedom, is a context in which praxis is "agglomerated into more consistent blocs" and in which it "pushes back symbols as a continent pushes back the sea that surrounds it."[15] As for Talcott Parsons, economic or instrumental rationality is for Dumont the element in modernity that is responsible for the erosion of traditional norms and for the failure to generate new *sens*: it is the factor that dynamizes and fragments social relations and, therefore, must be circumscribed in its deployment.

Even the classical and neo-classical economists have, in Dumont's view, had to acknowledge the need to recuperate *sens*, almost from the moment that they destroyed it by formulating their abstraction of "economic man" released from the intentionality towards the *avènement*. Indeed, all modern anthropologies show the dual movement of doubling the world by an abstraction that shears away from the context in which it is rooted and then doubles back to mend the rent by forging new relations with that context. That dialectical process has already been described for philosophy, which was thrown back on individual subjectivity by the emergence of specialized science and then constituted itself from that subjectivity as a criticism of the relations of man and man, and man and world. In the case of economics the remainder that had to be re-claimed was a sense of purpose for the totality. Classical economics first accomplished this recuperation through the notion of equilibrium, essentially a reification in which "mechanisms substitute for decisions." As the technological society became more clearly defined through the dominance of complex organizations and the self-conscious formation of contesting classes, and as economists sought to explain and prescribe for the new situation, the idea of equilibrium ceded to that of growth which involves acknowledgement of the con-sciousness of economic agents, of complexes of fina-lities, and, most importantly, of concrete temporality: History, as Dumont remarks, "fatally invaded" the field of economic thought.[16] But the efforts of eco-nomists to restore *sens* to the domain from which they had removed it are necessarily incomplete; insofar as their discipline is to remain distinctive it must be drawn towards its initiating act of liberating calculative reason, its intentionality towards the *événement*. Yet the histor-icization of economics evidences a far more general project of the recuperation of *sens* in modern anthro-pologies; that is, the study of history itself, and thus prepares economics for conciliation with other social sciences and with the other cultural practices to which it refers.

Each of the anthropologies that arise from the *dédoublement* of the primary culture that constitutes everyday life has a specificity with regard to the dis-closure it makes of the disarticulation of modern life and the contribution it might make to the restoration of *sens*. Philosophy, for example, reveals the vacant subjectivity of individuals who, stripped of secure meanings, seek to transcend themselves through their own void, but it also contributes the critique of the reifications of the disciplines that have pretended to supplant it. Economics indicates the social disintegra-tion brought about by the liberation of calculative reason from traditional normative constraints, but it leads to the utopia of self-conscious planning. However, while philosophy is paradigmatic for all the other anthropologies, because it has no standardized object or method, and economics is the discipline that best reveals the purport of modern rationalism, history is for Dumont perhaps the most important anthropology, because it holds the best promise for the recuperation of *sens.* History, more than the other anthropologies, is a direct response to the disarticulation of modern culture. In his essay "L'histoire à faire, l'histoire à écrire", Dumont poses the question of why history should have arisen as a science in the nineteenth century. He grounds the emergence of historical science in "three major modifications of the relations of Western man with his environment," all of them formative of the intentionality towards the *événement:* "the appearance of an acute sense of accelerated social changes, of which the import appeared to be uncertain; the emergence of new groups, such as nations and classes; the rearrangement of the conditions of political decision."[17] As a response to these modifications history arose as a way of conferring *sens* in an environment of uncertainty: its primal intention was not to explore the past for its own sake, but to give man a future. For Dumont, nineteenth-century man believed that human beings fashion their own relation to the world, rather than receiving it, as was the case for the man of tradition and myth, or finding it inscribed in nature, as was the case for the man of reason. Thus, nineteenth-century man turned to the past to discover how the world that he inhabited had been created: "to understand humanity, to give it a future supposes a deciphering of history."[18]

The healing function of history, its possibility of helping to integrate modern life, is evinced in the manner in which it places the *avènement* and the *événement* in dialectical relation. Historical science shares in the intentionality towards the *événement*, not only because its concern is with past happenings, but because it studies those events in terms of the constitutive activities of concrete human beings: "Beyond the *structures* which claim to be founded on functional and technical criteria, and which are the object of the systematic sciences, history recalls that there is always decision, uncertainty, choice."[19] Further, history effects its own *dédoublement* by engendering historiography, which brings the products of historical science themselves under the reign of the *événement*: "Among all the human sciences, historiography is the only discipline which has always affirmed that it was relative to the successive generations which interrogate history."[20] The hyper-relativization of historiography, which in turn relativizes historical science in a manner similar to that in which philosophy reduces reifications to horizons, would appear to effect further divisions in culture rather than to heal those already existing. But it is just that relativization which allows an opening for a modern equivalent of the *avènement*. Historiography reveals that behind the surface concern with events, the science of history is primarily attentive to the problems posed for conduct in successive presents; that is, history is the interpretation of the present in terms of the past undertaken by those who seek to emplace themselves in an uncertain future. Dumont does not mean to imply, however, that history is a collection of arbitrary viewpoints. In his essay "Idéologie et savoir historique", he notes that although historiography is "an ideology which admits of its own mechanism of debate," it is "in continuity with existence, which projects it towards rationalization." Its task is to "assimilate the facts of the past, but at the limit, the facts of the past are irreducible."[21] Here the special healing function of history becomes evident: it is a way of conferring *sens* to concrete situations that is disciplined by objectivity. Thus, it provides the basis for a community of interpretation that transcends partial and partisan perspectives without reducing them to a contrived unity.

History's substitute for the *avènement* is a continually

renewed dialogue about what man should become carried on in terms of what he has been. It replaces the appeal of traditional man to a fixed set of symbols and values that are understood to be pre-existent to human experience with recourse to an abundant and variegated past, different aspects of which are brought forward as new elements of the human situation become problematic and others are provisionally resolved. One might say that history creates the possibility of an open tradition, one not merely reformulated piecemeal and reluctantly in response to crises, but that is self-consciously and consistently reconstructed. Dumont, indeed, speaks in the language of tradition when he defines history's proper function in collective life: "Our problems and our crises are original questions to pose to the past, and the past is a living memory where heritages rejoin engagements."[22] History as a dialogue about man's definition of himself, then, is Dumont's variant of the quest of classical sociologists for a therapeutics based on social knowledge. Dumont's use of historiography as a relativizing mode of thought which simultaneously directs attention to the totality most resembles Mannheim's sociology of knowledge, which also relativized perspectives so that they could be composed with one another. In both cases the final appeal is to a reason that recognizes its limits in facticity and time, but that persists nevertheless in its search for conciliation.

Dumont's appeal to history as a way of restoring the past as a "living memory where heritages rejoin engagements" is undertaken in an era in which history itself is threatened with the loss of its social bases by the "society of operations." Dumont, indeed, acknowledges that there may be only a slender possibility today for history to perform its healing function. The complex organizations that dominate contemporary social life seek to do without historical dialogue and to substitute for it functional designs in the world of work and programmed consumption in the realm of leisure. In

Le Lieu de l'Homme Dumont notes that "documentation" increasingly replaces history in the human sciences and that it is not fanciful to predict that "in the near future the masters-of documentation will be the masters of history": "The archivist would be linked directly to the technocrat, expelling the historian and the politician." Dumont warns that the human sciences will be "dissolved" in documentalism altogether "unless they finally acknowledge that their constructions are, at bottom, only a recourse against what Hegel called 'bad subjectivity', that is, that these constructions are a placing of the subject once again in a judgement by which the subject examines itself about the history that makes it and that it contributes to remake."[23] The human sciences, in short, must become aware of the human need for *sens*.

4

Cultural Practices: Ideology and Religion

At present the standing of Fernand Dumont in the intellectual world is guaranteed primarily by his philosophy of the social sciences and particularly by the masterful dialectical analysis of anthropologies that he accomplished in his treatise *L'Anthropologie en l'Absence de l'Homme.* However, although Dumont has, indeed, devoted a major portion of his thought to the relations among the sciences of man and to their internal structures, to consider his work as centered in the philosophy of social science may reveal more about the contemporary intellectual world than it does about his most significant contributions. In terms of profession, Dumont is a sociologist and the primary audience for his work is composed of social scientists. According to Dumont's own analysis, they are participants in the *culture savante*, which in the modern period has split itself off from the more general or popular culture in order to constitute independent realms of discourse that tend to become self-enclosed and self-referential. It is intelligible, then, that Dumont's audience would be disposed to read his work in terms of their own concerns and even, ironically, to criticize him for giving too much weight to those concerns in his interpretation of modern history. But Dumont is far more than a philosopher of the social sciences or even than a theorist of culture, though the latter designation comes much closer to the mark. He is perhaps most justly understood as a *penseur*, after the fashion of such French Enlightenment figures as Voltaire and Diderot, who must practice his vocation in an era of specialization. The special contribution of the *penseur*, who stands between the Spanish *pensador* (essentially a versatile man of letters) and the Northern European scholar, is a criticism of life as a whole disciplined by conversance with science. Even less than the philosopher does the *penseur* have a determinate object or method to guide his investigations. In the contemporary intellectual world his integrative vision tends to get lost when too much attention is paid to the specialized studies in which it must be expressed. Yet it is just that vision, in Dumont's case the interplay of *sens* and *absence*, which is the *penseur's* cultural gift.

Dumont does not philosophize about the social sciences in a vacuum. They arise in, mirror, and attempt to inform and minister to a society which has become constituted by complex organizations that tend to form hermetic worlds and to erode more general cultural unities received from the past. Contemporary culture, for Dumont, is expressed on at least four planes, each of which intersects the others. First there is the learned culture, the *culture savante:* a reconstitution of more primary cultures according to specialized, individualized, or rationalized perspectives or postulations. Second, there are the cultural practices of differentiated institutions, such as law, religion, business, government, and education, that may utilize the schematisations of the *culture savante,* but cannot duplicate them as programs of action, since these practices must emplace man directly in an intricate web of social relations. Third, there is the popular culture of those who receive the effects of hierarchical organizations and who adapt to them by reworking traditional practices, appropriating the significations relayed by the mass media of communications, and generating significations of their own to express their aspirations. And finally there are the vestiges of the traditional unities of *sens*, which sustain themselves precariously in isolated social environments or are taken up by organizations and used pragmatically for merchandising or mobilization. Dumont's interest in the social sciences is guided by a concern for how they do and might interrelate with other contemporary cultural practices and forms. In particular he is disturbed by the way in which the social sciences tend to take as their object the institutionalized cultural practices of complex organizations and how, in turn, these organizations employ the findings of the social sciences to rationalize their practices even further. The reciprocal relation between the social sciences and organized cultural practices leaves out popular culture except as a datum to be reworked in systematizations or as a receptacle for programmed significations intended to incite specific behaviors. Dumont's overall aim is to redirect the social sciences towards aiding the emergence of a more unified and participatory popular culture that would become the reference for the other cultural practices, though it would not deprive them of their relative autonomy. Thus, his philosophy of the social sciences is an aspect of his general criticism of life.

Dumont has remarked in *L'Anthropologie en l'Absence de l'Homme* that "wishing to constitute himself as objective subject, the anthropologist had progressively to let Method substitute for him and therefore become the true subject of science." Yet the vacating of individual subjectivity, which necessarily created "Being" or

"Structure" as the object of the human sciences, was illusory. "After the procedures of desubjectivization, after the advent of Method, after Being and Structure, the author does not disappear. Man as subject is liquidated; the one who conducts the liquidation remains."[1] Contemporary anthropology proceeds, for Dumont, in the absence of man, but it is shadowed by the figure of the anthropologist. Such is also the case for Dumont's own thought, which is a self-conscious expression of "utopia" that provides coherence to objective analyses of cultural forms. As *penseur* Dumont does not approach the study of culture in the guise of technician or underlaborer, but from a confrontation with the conditions of his own existence. The shadow cast over his thought is that of a man who grapples personally with the tension in his being between his proletarian origins in Quebec and his destiny as contributor to the cosmopolitan *culture savante*; and publically with the agony of modernization in Quebec, the transition from traditional society to a form as yet undefined. The great breadth and intensity of Dumont's thought may in part be accounted for by his being simultaneously one who was caught up in rapid social change and who distanced himself sufficiently to observe that change. His social thought is serious because it runs beyond the expression of an academician's career to that of a personal existence confronting the tensions, uncertainties, misgivings, and hopes of a social revolution, Quebec's "Quiet Revolution" of 1960-1970.

The major themes of Dumont's thought become more intelligible in light of his position as exemplary participant in and analyst and critic of the "Quiet Revolution." It is in periods of rapid social change that the opportunity to be a *penseur* arises. And Dumont may be understood as the quintessential *penseur*, because his thought is defined by the struggle to find *sens* in and to confer it on the world, an engagement that is revealed to be fundamental when change is proceeding and its resolution cannot be foreseen clearly. The interplay of *sens* and *absence* is the predicament of one who exists in a revolutionary situation and senses the ruptures that it creates, seeking to preserve what is valuable in a vanishing past and to lay claim to a promise, a "dream of April" jeopardized by the possibility of a loss of cultural integrity. The *dédoublement* is similarly an expression of the disarticulation of a changing society and an unreconciled life, both of which stand between cultural systems, unable to integrate them. Cosmopolitan culture has infiltrated into Quebec, but it has not fully articulated itself in solidary relation with the dissipating traditional forms. It is in just this situation that the threat of a society of operations filling the cultural void with prefabricated mechanistic systems becomes most clearly manifest. And here the substantive features of Dumont's thought become concretely rooted. The various utopias that he proposes, all of which mediate between tradition and modernity (*avènement* and *événement*) are intelligible alternatives to operationalism in a social context that has not yet achieved routinization. Dumont may be understood profoundly as a man who has become ultra-modern, hyper-sophisticated, a success story of the Quiet Revolution, and who turns back to his origins both as a healer of his people and as a seeker after what he has lost in his journey in the wider world. His complex intentions and his protracted struggle to overcome his torment are illustrated nowhere better than in his studies of the more direct cultural practices, particularly ideology and religion, to which he has devoted sustained study.

The unity of Dumont's thought is superbly illustrated in his reflections on religion, in particular on the Catholic faith. Catholicism is, for Dumont, a total life concern; the deep, grounding, and enveloping commitment of his personal existence and, as that takes on expanse, of his social being. It is in his meditations on the "conversion of Christian thought" from a vacillation between the poles of legalism and individual spirituality to a cultural practice informed by transcendence that embraces all of the dimensions of human existence without sacrificing their autonomy that Dumont takes his fundamental stance towards the contemporary crisis, binding together his poetic vision of obstinate torment in a refractory world and his dialectic of *sens* and *absence* in the human sciences, "anthropology in the absence of man." Christianity, besides being Dumont's personal orientation towards the world, provides him with his primary mediation between provincialism and cosmopolitanism, Quebec and the global society of operations, giving him a link with universality that is solidary with his specific cultural inheritance. It is indicative of how careful Dumont is to distinguish the specificity of each variant of human thought and to confine his discussion to the field of discourse defined by its limits, that one would not know he is a Christian were one to study only his analyses of the sciences of man and of the cultural practices other than religion. Yet his Christian commitment silently leavens all of his reflections, leading him always to declare for the insufficiency of all modes of secular or profane thinking to grasp the totality of human concerns. Dumont's dialectics, indeed, may be understood, though certainly not exhaustively, because he does not engage in apologetics, as means of cultivating receptivity to the marvelous (*le merveilleux*) and of creating openings for a faith that would inform a complete life in the moving structure of technological society. The fundamental dialectic of *sens* and *absence* is itself a way of disposing oneself expectantly and vigilantly to receive faith, not as a passive vessel, but as an actor who must continually emplace himself in a life essentially unbalanced.

Dumont's reflections on Christianity appear in his book, *Pour La Conversion de la Pensée Chrétienne,* which comprehends all of the aspects of Catholic faith, moving from a consideration of the problem of religion in modern history, through an exposition of the Christian posture towards existence, to a vision of a renewed and reformed Christian life. In his comments on the position of the Church in modern times Dumont makes connection with his philosophy of history. Dumont's diagnosis of the problem of contemporary religion is based on the fragmentary character of the technological society, which splits the various phases of life into closed compartments. Catholicism has prolonged itself into modern times from its roots in traditional society, where it constituted the organizing center of the intentionality towards the *avènement*, providing human beings with the values and aspirations which gave *sens* to their concrete existence. In modern times, however, religion in general and the Church in particular have been displaced by the emergence into independence of other human activities, each of which has its own specificity, but all of which share in the impulse to rationalization. The rise of calculative reason has tended to make of religion "one zone of consciousness among others."[2] Yet religion cannot exist without stagnating if it is confined only to a corner of life; it must inform the entirety of consciousness without usurping the autonomy of the other zones. Indeed, the profane, which Dumont identifies with calculative reason, is always "a fragment that is set apart on the background of the sacred," because it is not possible for reason to "equal the totality of consciousness."[3] Dumont compares the sacred to the "landscape which serves as the pretext for the painter," which he opposes to "the terrain of which the engineer calculates the stability in order to put up an edifice." The sacred has not disappeared in modern times; it has been pushed back into a "layer that is superposed to existence, where its truth is concentrated in its lack of effectiveness."[4] There are still ultimate ends, but they are "clothed in a figure of nostalgia which has no way of taking on body in the real." The sacred, then, has suffered deprivation in technological society; modern religion is, in Heidegger's terms, a "privative form" of what it should be in its fullness.

The response of Christianity to being edged out of the society of operations has been a "profound scission" of the religious consciousness in broad strata of the Christian population: "The dislocation of existence, the partitioning of conducts that is characteristic of technical society, evidently plays against religion, which no longer diffuses itself, with tradition, through the whole of life. Religion tends also to become a closed universe, a type of conduct that is *juxtaposed* to the others."[5] In becoming "one cell among others" religion risks losing its root in human existence and falls prey to being an "artificial and foreign element in it." The uprooting of Christianity takes two forms that are derived from the fundamental split in modern life between objectivity and subjectivity. Institutionally, the Church responds to its displacement and to its disarticulation with other human activities by attempting to preserve its integrity by recourse to conformism, ritualism, and legalism; by closing itself off from the rest of society as a separate and rigid universe with its own rules, which fosters a "juridicalism" based on the "piety of fear." A "Christian culture" arises which is directed by the clerical hierarchy and which is at best a compensation for the discontinuities encountered by communicants in the other phases of their lives. From the side of subjectivity, as the counterpart to juridicalism, individuals cultivate a private "spiritualism" which has no contact with the tasks of public life and which encourages a sense of the self-sufficiency of personal consciousness. For Dumont, then, the Catholic consciousness is doubly divided in the contemporary world; first, it is split off as a whole from the profane, from the intentionality towards the *événement,* and, second, it is torn asunder within itself into organizationally induced conformism and privatized spiritualism.

Dumont places the origin of the "profound scission" of Christian consciousness in the Church's strategy of adapting to the liberation of the profane by assuming a defensive posture of making itself an inaccessible island in which its traditions might be preserved. As a consequence of its strategy the Church not only lost contact generally with the changes wrought by technological society, but specifically could not minister convincingly to the daily needs of emerging social classes, particularly the working class. The limitations of the Church's adaptation to modern times are nowhere more evident to Dumont than in Quebec, where the defensive posture was assumed in a general environment of imperialism. For Dumont, the case of Quebec is a "striking example of a Church in which initiative has been absorbed from top to bottom in the exercise of clerical power."[6] After British rule was imposed, the Church was "forced to maintain its existence in a country that was dominated by Protestant masters, for whom religion was besides in great part an affair of state." In response to imperialism, the Church exaggerated its protective strategy and made a policy of loyalty to the ruling powers in return for an allowance of autonomy over a circumscribed field of religious concerns. The result was that the Church not only "desolidarized itself with popular struggles for liberty, but deprived the people of all political education, save that which consisted of teaching to the good men, according to Msgr. Hubert's expression, 'a total submission to the whole legal system and the laws, with neither examination nor discussion.' "[7] The Church in Quebec, then, became an exemplary case of the general disposition of Catholicism to distance itself from modernity and to try to preserve a traditional form of life in a society increasingly dominated by calculative reason. The strategy was a failure because the Church's isolation was only apparent; its relative autonomy was guaranteed by a political pact that would make it irrelevant and finally adverse to the aspirations of the greater part of its communicants. It is with reference to the "desolidarization" of the Church hierarchy with the greater part of the faithful that Dumont proposes his "conversion of Christian thought."

By "the conversion of Christian thought" Dumont means its realignment from being a concern of the clerical hierarchy directed towards the more general Christian community to being a care of the entire community, including the hierarchy. But the renewal and reform that Dumont urges are not fundamentally structural; they take place in the depths of human existence first and then flow outwards into the social world. Dumont's philosophy of Christianity might best be called one of "Christian engagement," in which the believer, in concert with his fellows, heals the breach between juridicalism and spirituality by creating a community that informs action in the wider social world with the inspiration of the revealed Word. Dumont searches for a "conscious faith," based on acute questioning of and commerce with the profane, to replace the sense of the sacred that spontaneously leavened the secular life of traditional societies. The root of Christian engagement is found by Dumont in a theology of incarnation that is deeply existential. He states that we have been "placed in the world to open painstakingly all the secret folds of the sense of Mystery, not in order to create in ourselves a sort of yawning abyss, with blurred outlines, where faith would fall as a massive response; but to look towards testing faith with this flesh which, for man, creates his distance in relation to God and makes him, in fact, an irreplaceable respondant."[8] The flesh, for Dumont, takes on a comprehensive significance, including not only each one's body, but also "the world which puts men face to face": "The flesh is continued in the vast social constructions that we erect to join us together in common ideals."[9] The flesh, however, is not a self-sufficient totality. Indeed, the incarnation of Christ is a delay (*délai*) before being a reconciliation, "a delay so that the reconciliation is worthwhile." History is discontinuous, as is the whole fleshly world of the profane: "The profane is a *corner* which blocks the fluency of our representations of the supernatural and which permits us, therefore, to make our questioning of man profound."[10] There is no "cheap grace," to use Dietrich Bonhoeffer's term, in Dumont's Christianity. Christ gives a promise, but we are not in direct communion with God. Here the attitude of obstinate torment that informed Dumont's poetry becomes the core of his religious vision. We are profoundly disarticulated with the world, but must seek in it the signs of and the paths to our redemption.

As a way of overcoming the contemporary scission of Christian consciousness, Dumont's theology of incarnation and engagement is founded on a subtle dialectic that places in delicate opposition and reciprocity the demands of faith for absolute commitment and the perplexities, absences, of the world of the flesh. Christianity, for Dumont, is not one ideology among others, but a "Sign raised among the nations": "The Christian and the Church are syntheses *a priori* of the human condition."[11] Christian engagement, for Dumont, does not reject these syntheses, which in his view would be the true object of the intentionality towards the *avènement,* but is "the slow and precarious discovery of the *a posteriori*." Although, as he confronts the world, the Christian is a laborer who is "sure of his vocation," the field that he tills is "fallow" and he must learn his *métier* once again each day. Human existence is a "long condemnation to the profane" and the Christian has no itinerary already traced for him to lead him through it: "The risk of the Christian presence to the world is the first condition of our engagement."[12] The project of discovering the *a posteriori*, of opening the folds of the sense of Mystery in the extended and disjointed world of the flesh must be based on the "free engagement" of each Christian, which is the replacement in Dumont's converted Christian thought for the isolated "Christian culture" propounded by the clerical hierarchy. That engagement, however, is not void of content but gains direction from the basic concerns of contemporary human existence. Man today wishes to be liberated from the imposed and calculated programs of life devised by the society of operations. Yet he also seeks a more rational society which does not repose on arbitrary privileges and which is a convergence of the highest intentions of human beings, "an image of their friendship," rather than a "vast system of the division of labor, a simple means for the satisfaction of economic needs."[13] A Christian thought converted to engagement can, for Dumont, provide a way towards this utopia, because it does not reject the intentionality towards the *événement* but embraces the total world of the flesh by appropriating the spirit of technology; that is, its self-consciousness, and, thereby, leading technology beyond itself and giving it a spiritual dimension now only incipient in it.

As Christian engagement flows outward to confront the wide expanse of the flesh it takes on a social dimension that involves relations to dynamics that are not rooted in Christianity and that have often been adverse to it. Indeed, the Church itself is permeated by the profane world and exists as a structure which both comes to the world from outside as "Christ diffused and communicated," and inserts itself into the vicissitudes of history. In order to make Christian engagement effective, the Church must be rethought in such a way that it can minister to the needs of the broader society and heal the rifts within itself. For Dumont, the free engagement of the Christian consciousness has its fruit not in the dispersed activities of individuals, but in the reconstitution of Christian society around the "People of God." As the milieu in which the Christian mystery is communicated, the Church determines "an economy of revelation composed of tradition and hierarchy." The "Christian people" is assembled by the Mystery through the mediation of the hierarchy. In his conversion of Christian thought, Dumont rejects the traditional interpretation of the People of God as a "congregation of the faithful" (*Congregatio fidelium*), which is too restrictive to meet the requirements of a

Christian community in a differentiated and divided society, in favor of the idea of a "convocation," which designates "my belonging to the People of God as distinguished from my other allegiances."[14] Dumont does not propose to eliminate the hierarchy, which he believes is essential to Christian society, but to bring the hierarchy into reciprocity with the believers, thereby revivifying such institutions as the parish and allowing them to enrich other solidarities that foster fraternal aid. As a mediation between legalism and private spirituality, between the sacred and the profane, and between the Church and the world, the convocation of Christians is self-consciously open to the dynamics and variegated interests of technological society, but is also drawn towards its unique gift of the revealed Word. Dumont, following in the line of Durkheim, rejects "all possibility of a community founded on similitude" and suggests that only "a community based on complementarity," which must find its focus in response to the spiritual needs of contemporary life, is adequate to sustain Christian engagement. Dumont does not prescribe a program for such a community, but provides a form in which the Church might find its way back to a solidary relation with its communicants and conduct its mission as a "Sign raised among the nations."

If Dumont's Christian community does not have a detailed plan of action, it does have a formal coherence that is gained through the historicity of the Church. Dumont remarks that as a "living organism" the Church has been loath to define its past systematically, because "its Truth is in history in an altogether different fashion than are philosophies or ideologies: as the expansion of a presence, as a ferment which manifests its truth by its fecundity."[15] The focus of the historical consciousness of the Church is the People of God: "It is this community, which, confronted with the uncertainties of the present, must decipher freely its *sens* in solidarity with the reading of its past."[16] Here

Dumont brings forward again the healing and mediating function of history. Although the convocation of Christians is assured, through its faith, of the "continuity of its presence in history," it must give itself precise representations of its past, none of which can be "furnished officially and once and for all." In a Christian thought that has been converted to a practice of self-conscious engagement, the Christian community has recourse to the *culture savante* which provides it with historical criticism. Just as in the profane society the historian carries on the task of perpetually reinterpreting the past in light of present demands and aspirations, so the specialist in positive theology and the Church historian are delegated by the community to provide representations of its past which are referred neither to a pre-existent system of interpretations nor to a purely personal experience of the present, but to the needs of the People of God in light of received tradition: "(They) translate tradition into an explicit memory."[17] As a cultural practice Christianity shares, with all of the others, despite its uniqueness for Dumont, a dialectical structure that moves from operation, through action, to interpretation; here specifically from juridicalism, through engagement, to historicization. Through this dialectic the rents in modern society might be mended and in the case of Christianity the *sens* received *a priori* might be given flesh: "An authentic spirituality appears to us as one which accepts being situated between the *a priori* of tradition and the spontaneity of personal consciousness, in order to trace from the one to the other the roads of conversion that are ceaselessly retaken."[18]

Dumont's Christianity is not a happy one, though it is informed by the hope for community. The idea of a "convocation" is for Dumont himself a compromise and a concession wrenched from the rentings of his being, an admission that the Church cannot be the sole granter of *sens* to man in a world that seems to have fallen into hopeless fragmentation. Commitment to the convocation is in distinction from Dumont's other attachments, perhaps even opposed to them, though the liberated convocation would embrace technological society in order to spiritualize it. Dumont is a Christian, but a tragic one who looks more to the way through the world than to the salvation beyond it, though he is faithful, because reconciliation has been delayed by our "condemnation to the profane." As freely engaged Christians, the members of the convocation must enter into ceaseless dialogue to knit together their fragmented experiences into a mission. Each one must struggle to make *sens* on his own account of each day's work, though he must also submit to tradition, and there is no guarantee that the various contributions of individual *sens* will make a garment of culture. Dumont has remarked that liberalism, the "mother of all the other ideologies," had made of "dispersed individuals a collectivity of schizophrenics."[19] We live in the wash of that schizophrenia, the society of operations expressed by anthropologies in the absence of man. But we are still flesh-and-blood human beings; indeed, the world itself is an extension of the flesh. And we cannot be dead to the flesh, to a fragmented world: our mission is to discover the *a posteriori.* So we must try to make *sens* in concert, as best we can. A convocation could in the present day be only one focus of *sens* among many, some of the others of which lay legitimate claim on the believer. Though it might not itself be guided by an ideology, but by an *a priori* synthesis, it would enter a world of ideological formations, because ideology is the failed substitute in a fragmented world for the intentionality towards the *avènement.* Ideology is *sens* backed by power, not by faith, the expression of a world of conflict which gives substance to Dumont's concluding remarks in *Pour la Conversion de la Pensée Chrétienne* that the mission of the Christian people will have to be marked by "much groping and much suffering."[20] The social world as an extension of the flesh expresses incoherence as conflict, and in a world of conflict ideologies both ameliorate and exacerbate the chaos. The Christian convocation must be tormented as well as hopeful; the pieces of meaning are scattered; they can be fit together no longer.

The modern world as we know it, for Dumont, begins in the void created by liberalism, which was the ideological expression of the bourgeoisie, the bearers of rationalization in the world. According to liberalism, society could be a concourse of contracting individuals; but, of course, that could never be because human life is constitutively social in the sense that it sustains itself through networks of collaboration. The fact of language itself, which appears to each individual as transcendent to his own uses of it (except in the case of the schizophrenic), is enough to refute the liberal view of man. Society is real, even if not personal; it has organization, even if it lacks coherence. As socially organized beings, men filled liberalism's *absence* with fragments of *sens* based on their special belongings. The *absence* has been covered with a profusion of conflicting *sens*, but it persists in the gaps opened up by the conflict. Ideology is inherently polemical because it expresses the engagements of the fragments of society with each other in terms of contesting images of the totality. Each ideology creates a world of *sens*, a *dédouble-ment* of a more primary conscious life, for its adherents, but that world does not exhaust the possibilities of interpretation. Indeed, Dumont remarks that "rather than masking contradictions and conflicts," ideology allows those conflicts to be seen "on the horizon of a hypothetical totality."[21] Ideology is hopelessly equivocal; it can be grasped at once as a pitiful effort of men to make *sens* out of their fragmented condition, a movement to heal that condition; and as a vehicle of concentrations of power to impose a partial interpretation of the totality on the other parts of society and on the person. Totalitarianism is a real threat for Dumont, the sense of the sacred captured in the toils of bureaucracy; but men are constituted by the struggle to acknowledge in and confer *sens* on their situations, and ideologies, rather than being false beliefs, as liberalism's self-delusion would have it, are their characteristic products in the technological society. They are the materials out of which our fragile and finite reconciliations are made.

Ideology, as the outgrowth of *sens* from the rationalization of the world, is not primarily a form of cognizing the world but a cultural practice that expresses men's aspirations in concrete situations by tying the former to definitions of the situation and plans of action. Indeed, all thought for Dumont is a translation of desire into definition, even if that desire is to know certain things in certain ways. Ideology places the stress on desire because it responds to the need of men to emplace themselves directly in the world through their comportment towards the discontinuous particulars of concrete existence; it is "a definition of the situation in view of action."[22] And that definition is self-consciously produced, which means that it cannot provide the security of the intentionality towards the *avènement* but must pretend to do so nonetheless; that is, to breed matrices of symbols and values that might give the illusion of transcendence. Ideology, then, is as clear an expression of the *imaginaire* as is literature, and it reveals that all other forms of thought, though they deny it, are also products of the *dédoublement*, not replicas of the object. Consciousness, for Dumont, is "*work*, work on desire": "It effectuates a transposition, a transmutation of what is simultaneously the attraction and the position of the object, *value* and *fact*."[23] Ideology does a more primary work on desire than does human science which enters a world of ideological significations on which it works. The profusion of ideologies from human engineering, which fills the gap of *sens* created by mechanization with a mechanistic view of man, to the programs and practices of higher education is grounded in the proliferation of specialized organizations and the various aggregations of men set apart by the situations that these organizations create. Ideology has suppressed more spontaneous and primary social unities of *sens* and has left in their place a Spencerian struggle to define the totality in which organized and hierarchical power-concentrations tend to prevail, even as they claim to be acting in terms of purely technical considerations: the ideology that proclaims the end of ideology.

On the other side of the Christian community, Dumont returns in his study of cultural practice to the social sciences as special practices of healing breaches. Here he addresses the possibility of a sociology constituted as a "socio-analysis of ideologies," which would not seek a synthesis of ideologies, since it would be an interrogation of how the *"practical syntheses"* that constitute society are fabricated; but would put the investigator's own social experience into play for the purpose of providing reintegrations of dispersed meanings. The objectivity of such a sociology would be secured, for Dumont, by admission of a "pluralism" of social experiences and by applying to the descriptions of experience the criterion of "the *fecundity* of the analyses that they permit," their possibilities of conferring coherent *sens*.[24] Thus sociology's object would be the "conflict of practices of interpretation," which Dumont considers to be "an operational definition of society."[25] Dumont's socio-analyst would perform a similar role to those of the historian and the philosopher, the provision of more generous and adequate projections of *sens* than are extant and the recovery of more spontaneous worlds of *sens* that have been effaced or hidden by ideological projections. As an alternative to power, a "sociology of mediation" must make contact with the popular culture. And at the end of his work on ideology, *Les Idéologies,* Dumont says: "The question could be led back to this: what conditions would be necessary in our societies for historical subjects to be able themselves to practice the hermeneutics of ideology, which science seeks to place in focus for its own use?"[26]

5
<hr>

Technology and Utopia

When Fernand Dumont's reflections on contemporary anthropologies are considered as a whole, they yield a description of the fundamental dynamics and possibilities of modern culture and society. Throughout Dumont's special studies there is in operation a dialectic that interrelates the primary factors that constitute modern life. The leading role in that dialectic is played by reason, in the privative form of modern rationalism, which effectuates a split in human life between interior and exterior, between a spontaneous subjectivity, which is divested of content, and a mechanistic interpretation of objectivity, which leads on to the self-conscious programming of the various phases of life through the vehicle of material, social, and cultural technologies. The rationalization of the world is expressed in the confrontation of empty subjectivity and functional objectivity, both void of *sens*, which progressively gives way to the encroachment on the self of an operational society, divided into conflicting fragments, depriving it increasingly of independent initiative. Through rationalization, the traditional society, based on intentionality towards the *avènement*, is destroyed and along with it the popular culture that it organized and informed but did not exhaust. But, lacking the ability to confer *sens*, scientific rationality must attempt to give some purpose to existence that it split apart, so it binds itself to the aims declared by the concentrations of functionalized power created by the social formations that bear and utilize rationalistic methods in the service of partial interests. As the contemporary world presently stands, then, the three interrelated factors of instrumental reason, popular culture, and power form the structure in which the possibilities for the transformation of modern life arise. Currently the general direction of modern life is towards the increasing solidarization of the strict relation between technical reason and organized power, and the complete voiding of popular culture and its replacement by forms of human engineering utilizing the symbols and values of tradition in pragmatic schemes of merchandising and mobilization. The society of operations, however, cannot generate an authentic totality because it has no means of reconciling the specialized and competing sectors of life, short of totalitarianism which imposes a fabricated set of values and symbols by terror and technique on the disjointed whole. Left to itself, the society of operations tends either to compound its own fragmentation or to force the pieces together into an untenable and coercive unity.

Cité de la liberté

The disarticulated condition of contemporary human existence cries out, in Dumont's view, for utopia; that is, for the vision of a future life that would overcome concretely and intelligibly the ruptures induced by instrumental rationality and enforced by organized power. His own path toward utopia is a conversion of reason from its service to hierarchical organizations and their elites to a reciprocal relation with a revivified popular culture and its bearers, the people, or man in the flesh considered in all its extension. The possibility of such a conversion, however, depends upon a transformation of reason itself, which has already occured, at least in part, in those disciplines of the *culture savante*, such as philosophy, history, and interpretative sociology, that have emerged in the modern period as practices aimed at recuperating what has been despoiled by the functional order. The healing disciplines are, for Dumont, already in place; he is not a visionary proposing a *nuovo scienza*, but a seeker after grounded options. His task has been to show how a proper understanding of the mediating disciplines could direct them with greater coordination and self-consciousness towards the revitalization of popular culture and of community. A renewed popular culture expressed in the form of a *cité de la liberté* would have to share in both the self-conscious responsibility at the core of the intentionality towards the *événement* and in a respect for multiple traditions that would take the place of the lost intentionality towards the *avènement*. The mediating reason of philosophy, history, and interpretative sociology provides the explicit design for an open community in which men continually reconsider the past in order to find a basis for achieving their aspirations in concert with one another. The practitioner of recuperative reason neither dictates plans to the people nor constructs self-sufficient visions of a good life, but attempts to clarify the possible import of the tendencies at work in modern life, thereby contributing clarification to the relatively incoherent strivings of the people and, thus, making those strivings more self-conscious.

Dumont has not merely urged human scientists to

become mediators, but has performed the healing role in his own concrete circumstances, the society of Quebec. It is, indeed, in his engagement with Quebec that his deep concern with man as an animal who utters his existence, his view of the potentiality of the social sciences to inform popular culture, and his commitment to free Christian engagement find their fruition. For he has approached Quebec as historian and historiographer, sociologist, and philosopher, always seeking not only to mend the rents in his own being between the cosmopolitanism of the refined *dédoublement* (the figure of Gaston Bachelard) and the provincialism of silent tradition (the image of Philippe Dumont), but to carry his own personal struggles into the public domain by attempting to give voice to the past, present, and future of his people. For Dumont, the interpreter of a society must finally rely for the basis of his initiatives on his own experience of a milieu that is already infected with *sens*, not on a pure observation of fact: "If positivistic rationalism can believe that it *perceives* or *observes*, a sociology that is thoughtful about the prefabrication of the social field can only start from this postulate: I do not see the social, I have experience of it."[1] Dumont has situated himself as a social being in Quebec by reaching into the depths of his own experience of his society and informing it with careful historical and sociological investigations. He is neither an apologist for the Quebec of the past, which adapted to the imposition of modern imperialism by closing itself off from self-conscious responsibility, nor a proponent of a technocracy that would merge Quebec into the global society of operations, but the philosopher of a Quiet Revolution that aspires to recuperate a forgotten and often silent past in order to forge a future integrity in which the technological society is limited and utilized by a genuine community founded in a popular culture given principle by an interpretative dialogue.

The Nihilistic Core

As historian and historiographer Dumont's project has been to uncover the roots of the emergence of the French Canadians as a self-conscious people and, by examining them, to diagnose the contemporary crisis of Quebec in terms of the basic framework in which the Québécois have conceived of their destiny, have given *sens* to themselves. Dumont's reflections are distilled in his essay "De l'idéologie à l'historiographie: le cas Canadien-français," which is on a par with and recalls such classical studies in the historical sociology of knowledge as Leopoldo Zea's *Positivism in Mexico* and Mannheim's *Conservative Thought.* For Dumont, the decisive event in the formation of Quebec national consciousness was the rebellion of 1837, which, in the wake of its suppression by the British, led both to the awakening of reflection on the meaning of Quebec as a historical entity and to an adaptation to defeat marked by the self-enclosure of Quebec society centered around the dominance of the Church hierarchy, the mystique of rural life, and the careerism of the middle class and small political elites, their terms of peace with an overwhelming commercial and industrial imperialism. Prior to 1837 Quebec had passed through two historical periods, those of French and of British rule. As a colony of France, prior to 1760, Quebec had been generally neglected, except as a field for the fur trade. In the shadow of "the sporadic interest of the Metropole for the colony" a genuine "folk-society" based on subsistence agriculture and "personal relations of a very great intensity" gradually took shape.[2] That society did not take explicit consciousness of itself, but, as is the case for traditional societies, accreted its characteristic folkways in the light of the intentionality towards the *avènement*, here provided by Catholicism. In the years following the British conquest the folk-society was generally prolonged, but under the changed conditions of the weakening of its secular elites: "the bourgeoisie is evicted from the fur trade by the British merchants;" the landowners, "who never had been very powerful, see their prestige decline even more;" and "the Church progressively becomes the most important power."[3] By the turn of the nineteenth century a new class rooted in the liberal professions had emerged, which at first was "accepted by the people as its natural spokesman," because its members were "sons of the people" who retained the "attitudes of the peasantry from which they issued."[4] By 1830, however, the new bourgeoisie had consolidated sufficiently to fall into opposition with the alliance of the Church and the British rulers, and to make a bid for constitutional reform under the banner of liberal ideology and republicanism. But the bourgeoisie had neither sufficient economic power to challenge British imperialism nor sufficient ties with the general population to stimulate their support. The failure of the rebellion of 1837 revealed the "paradoxical situation" of this class which was "linked to the people by its origins and by a remarkably egalitarian social structure," but which had to project itself in "a vision of the world without roots in the whole of this society" in order to carry on its struggles.[5] "A world without roots"; this was to be the nihilistic core at the centre of the Quebec vision in the modern age.

The results of the defeat of 1837 were the rise to supremacy of the clerical elite in Quebec society and the general adjustment of the bourgeoisie to the terms of British rule. Until the Quiet Revolution of 1960 Quebec society did not seek integration with modernity, but accepted externally induced economic transformation while attempting to preserve its traditional life by an acute consciousness of its difference: traditional society ceded to defensive nationalism. But the failure of the bourgeoisie to assume leadership of the society had another fruit, the awakening of historical consciousness. The ground of historiography in Quebec was the situation of the bourgeoisie in the 1840s: "In sum, in the face of the collapse of the ideals proposed by the older generation, confronted by a profound crisis of the structures of traditional society, and cut off from the new paths that will soon be opened by industrialization, the elite of the 1840s gives itself a definition of its present and future."[6] Their new ideology was a theoretical justification of the traditional society, based on the nostalgia for rural virtue and crowned with the doctrine of a special religious "vocation of the French race in America;" a "retreat to the early times of French domination, far back enough for dream to find again reality and security."[7] It was in this ideological climate that François-Xavier Garneau originated the tradition of historiography in Quebec through his *Histoire du Canada*. Garneau was a historian, not an ideologist, whose response to the defeat of 1837 was to "surmount the loss by making the nation live in universal memory."[8] He wished to express his hopes for a free nation through appeal to "historical facts." Garneau's historical interpretation was not a retreat to traditionalism, but a prolongation of the liberal ideology tempered by conservatism. Indeed for Dumont, Garneau "appears to have surmounted the antinomy" of liberalism and conservative romanticism by performing "a decisive transmutation: what until then, in bourgeois ideology, was constitutional or political liberty, he translated into liberty of the people."[9] For Garneau, the history of French Canada was a ceaseless struggle of the people for national conservation, first, in the period of French rule, against the Indians and the British colonies, and, second, in the era of British rule, against the new masters in political and parliamentary conflicts. Garneau's legacy was to "transmute, without apparent break, the bourgeois consciousness of his time into a national consciousness." His "people" was the "race" ("he does not evoke the concrete life of the common man"); his politics parliamentary. But though he considered the ideology of a class as the "consciousness of the whole people" he founded a tradition of self-conscious reflection on the past that might inform hopes for the future and that linked the aspirations of the 1830s to the realities of the 1840s: he performed the historian's healing function.

Bourgeois Nationalism

For Dumont, Quebec still lives in the shadow of the post-1837 commitments, though the Quiet Revolution began to move beyond them. In particular Garneau's interpretation of the French-Canadian people is still the point of orientation for the more direct cultural practices, especially politics. In his essay "L'étude systématique d'une société globale" Dumont argues that Garneau's design has inspired all of the textbooks up to the present and even historical research: "In effect, the period of our history which followed the constitutional struggles has not been replaced for our historians by an original problematic. One has rather, in certain cases, protracted the earlier problem, which is why we know more about the struggles for separate schools than about the processes of urbanization and industrialization."[10] The consequence of ignoring the radical transformations in Quebec society has been that historiography in French Canada has "taken on a systematic character which appears to distance it from our situations and our questions of today": "The pluralism of explanations is inherent to the historical consciousness when it wishes to be the replacement for tradition, but, in this country, history and tradition coexist in a troubling syncretism"[11] Here Dumont's criticism mirrors his analysis of the Church and of the bourgeoisie: in each case there has been a retraction into a fixed and enclosed universe that suffers change, but does not respond to it with ready and informed engagement. Dumont acknowledges the part played by imperialism in provoking this defensive adaptation (here his thought links up with contemporary dependency theory), but he is more profoundly an internal critic of his people, calling upon them to create the terms on which they might fully engage themselves in and with the technological society, because if they fail to do so they will be overrun by it. Those terms would not renounce completely the received tradition of historiography; indeed, Dumont's own conception of early French-Canadian society as a folk-society is a reworking of the ideas of the 1840s; but they would convert that tradition into an expression of the aspirations of the people, considered as concretely situated and not as "race." Dumont's own historiography takes up the motive of national conservation, but places it in dialectical relation with the encroachment of the rationalization of the world on Quebec. It is in response to the compromise formations of the 1840s that his own historiography develops.

Saint-Jérôme

What became of Quebec in light of the post-1840's compromise formation, in which the French-Canadian people maintained their will to distinctiveness by falling back on themselves, shielded by the Church hierarchy and articulated, at a distance, with rationalistic imperialism by a careerist bourgeoisie devoted to government service, is examined by Dumont concretely in his work of empirical and interpretative sociology, *L'Analyse des Structures Sociales Régionales: Étude sociologique de la région de Saint-Jérôme,* written with Yves Martin. Published in 1963, Dumont's study in regional sociology is a work of the Quiet Revolution that synthesizes his major concerns – Christian reform, socio-analysis, popular culture, and participatory cultural practice – in terms of the particular situation of his own people. *L'Analyse* grew out of a charge by Msgr. Emilien Frenette, Bishop of St.-Jérôme, to the Research Center of the Faculty of Social Sciences at Laval University to undertake a sociological study in his Diocese with the aim of informing a diocesan mission somewhat on the lines suggested by Dumont's reflections on the conversion of Christian thought. Dumont and Martin conceive of regional sociology as a study of the "structuration," by socio-cultural dynamics, of a human space that is coordinate with the temporal perspectives provided by history; indeed, regional sociology is the analogue, for the investigation of the present, to history which makes *sens* of the past. The authors propose, through the methods of empirical (demographic and informational-questionnaire) analysis and interpretation ("seizure of the concrete landscape"), to "give an account of the concrete life of men in a region of our country," prescinding from "traditional generalizations" and recuperating the "everyday" and "prosaic" existence of the inhabitants rather than the "habitual ideological reveries."[12] They wish to draw "nearer to these little incessant combats out of which ideologies are born – and (to be) more faithful to the primary intentions of sociology;" that is, "not symply to identify resources or even the economic poles of development, but also to know, for each unity of space, the attitudes of the population towards their own problems and the points of support and the obstacles that the social organization offers to a planning that is both democratic and efficacious."[13] Regional sociology is the mediation between history and utopia.

L'Analyse may be read as an essay in the application of dependency theory or, perhaps, better in the creation of a dependency theory through a concrete case analysis. The Diocese of St.-Jérôme is a dependency of Montreal, which in turn is a dependency of North American Anglo-imperialism. From the vantage point of the doubly-dependent periphery Dumont and Martin are able to grasp what had happened to Quebec over more than a century of having existed under the constraints of its compromise formation. They divide the Diocese into ten "micro-cultures," each of which is characterized by a specific form of economic life, and then show what kinds of social organization have expressed and informed this life. The authors find that despite variations in industrial development, urbanization, and agricultural wealth the Diocese is generally characterized by an "incoherent" social organization in which voluntary associations are wcak, few initiatives for improvement are taken by the population (even by its elites), and there is little concern with public services, especially with education, and with directing the effects of change self-consciously: "Saint-Jérôme is the pole of a vast territory of feeble structure."[14] The hallmarks of Saint-Jérôme are the fragmentation of groups (workers, farmers, businessmen, and professionals), their inability to cooperate with one another and the persistence of mutual suspicions towards each other, and, more deeply, a cultural void bespeaking the lack of a will to confront and to try to manage change. It is as though the substance of the traditional society that the compromise formation of the 1840s had intended to retrieve had been eroded by industrialization, the metropolitanization of Montreal, and the infiltration of the society of operations throughout the Province, and that nothing but obstinate torment had filled its place. The St.-Jérôme described by Dumont and Martin is an *absence*, suffused by the heavy silence of a dispirited people who turn their great fortitude towards sheer persistence, that which is left when Garneau's great project, "national conservation," is finally voided of anything to conserve. St.-Jérôme is the most concrete reference in Dumont's work for the *absence*. As the authors conclude about one of the micro-cultures: "... the people are delivered to multiple contradictory processes. This phenomenon must be placed in relation with an inevitable absence of a sentiment of belonging to a common destiny."[15]

As an example of the independent invention of dependency theory, here out of the morphological sociology of the French School (Durkheim's "material substrate of societies") and American human ecology (Robert E. Park's and Ernest W. Burgess's "adaptation of man to his milieu" through a "struggle for existence"), *L'Analyse* has the special feature of emphasizing internal criticism over the critique of external power. Although the authors acknowledge that, since the 1870s, Montreal has been "the pivot of the global ecological processes" transforming the Diocese and the Province as a whole, they believe that it is too simple to blame Montreal and the wider system of North American imperialism for the incoherence of social organization. The failure of initiative by the local population and especially by its elites and the elites of the Province is of far more serious concern to them, even if, as a causative factor, it can be explained as an adaptation to a more primary cause. The absence of solidarity in St.-Jérôme is so yawning that Dumont and Martin do not believe that the people themselves can take control of their destiny on their own: "The pattern of double occupation, the proximity of disparate cultural strata, the division between the generations, etc. make it evidently difficult to achieve a taking of consciousness of the situation which could open the way for adequately taking charge of it."[16] Change towards a more participatory and self-directive culture must first be initiated from the outside, with the intent of achieving democratic planning; economic planning at the level of the state "will have to be accompanied by a true cultural planning."[17] Such planning would have to proceed from the Provincial level, the focus of a *politique des ensembles*, and would make the centers of each region, such as the city of St.-Jérôme, which hitherto have not assumed leadership over development, strong mediators (*relais*) between the metropolis and the towns and rural areas. The authors consider failure at the Provincial level to be the "capital problem." If the regional city is to become "truly the pivot of diversification and unity" (and by extension of tradition and technology), rather than a contributor to disorganization, an exemplar of social incoherence, a broader taking of consciousness will be necessary.

The Quiet Revolution: Ecstacy or Suicide?

Dumont makes his own contribution to a "taking of consciousness of the situation which could open the way for adequately taking charge of it" in his work of political philosophy and social criticism, *The Vigil of Quebec,* which was published in 1971, just after the FLQ crisis and the invocation of the War Measures Act by the federal government. The events of 1970 recall those of 1837. In both cases a movement by the Quebec society led by certain of its sectors to redefine itself economically, culturally, and politically met a limit of the environing power system and was left with a need to consider the destiny of the Province more self-critically and self-consciously. *The Vigil of Quebec* is explicitly intended to facilitate this process of taking stock, which Dumont had considered to be imperative long before 1970, as is evidenced by *L'Analyse*. He seeks in *The Vigil* to find a way for the Quiet Revolution to be continued, to avoid the retrenchment that had characterized the previous adaptation to power and to stimulate the emergence of a more coherent and democratic society. Here he is no longer primarily historian or sociologist but philosopher and, as the criticism of reification implies, proto-ideologist, defending a social and democratic nationalism: "I am concerned less with isolating the forces at work than with looking for the attitudes I ought to adopt as I confront the destiny of that fragile community which is my own."[18] Dumont seeks to emplace himself in his situation by making *sens* of its public dimension. His questions are those of the utopian tempered by the realization of the need to recur to the past in order to project a future that is concretely possible, a live option: "Is there any meaning in this history, this vigil of a paradoxical people? Is it worth keeping up?"[19] Dumont responds to these questions as a defender of his people, urging them towards the project of an "experimental society" devoted to constituting community in a technological order rather than to vacillating between immersion in the society of operations and romantic and particularistic nationalism, the retreat to the Golden Age prior to 1760. Based on an attempt by Dumont "to stand on that hypothetical spot where our personal existence and the collective life that concerns us more closely can be reconciled and understood as one," *The Vigil* shows the contribution that the Dumontian philosopher makes to public existence.

The Vigil is fundamentally an interpretation of the Quiet Revolution. For Dumont its essence was, paradoxically, to shatter the tormented silence of Quebec, to fill the void of *sens* left by the compromise formation of the 1840s with a plethora of diverse and often clashing utterances: Quebec society was finding its voice and, understandably, had become confused about its meaning and its future. In the "Letter to my English-Speaking Friends," which introduces the English translation of *The Vigil* Dumont remarks: "Since we decided to cease being what we were, it is comprehension of what we want to be that is required of you." But, "we would first have to know what it is that we want to be."[20] The only way, for Dumont, that a society that has changed drastically ("from at least seeming religious solidarity to rapid dechristianization, from ignorance to mass education, from Duplessis to independentism, from the challenges of *Cité libre* to the tutelage of Trudeau") can reattach itself to a lost past and project itself towards a future under its control is to utter itself: "After so much silence and so much stammering, we have at least one certain duty: to speak out."[21] The Quiet Revolution, then, is at its deepest root an attempt to give *sens* to a situation, as clear an attempt as could be documented, because it had been preceded by the silence of the repressed: "A people in tutelage from their beginning, whose public face constantly hid more confused experiences and desires, has attempted self-expression by every means and all at the same time."[22] Coherence of expression can only be achieved through "this agony of utterance." Dumont's aim is to help form this coherence through projecting a general design for Quebec's future based on his historical and sociological understanding, to perform the healing function of mediating reason: he would turn the cries from the void and into the night of the society of operations into the dialogue of a living community, a community of spirit informing flesh. The "largely artificial prosperity Quebec experienced after the last world war" had "brought disorder to needs and aspirations that had long flowed in stable channels," and the Quiet Revolution was the response to that disorder, the first effort of the French-Canadian people to articulate a destiny for themselves.

The Quiet Revolution had fanned the "live coals of the world" that Dumont evokes in his poetry into a blaze. The problem in 1970 was to control that blaze so that it would keep burning and would not be extinguished, either by the powers of rationalized organization or the people themselves fearing their own possibilities and seeking to return to a past compromise that was no longer viable. For Dumont, the Quiet Revolution was essentially "a cultural revolution," which left economic and political changes for the future. He concentrates in *The Vigil* on addressing those economic and political changes, rooting his proposals for socialism and democracy in Quebec nationalism. Dumont believes that in light of its "agony of utterance" the French-Canadian people need "some form of independence" so that they can be able to constitute themselves in self-conscious dialogue with the Anglo-Canadians, the other people "north of the United States," neither of whom has "so far found a genuine way to cooperate and effectively check the hold of their neighbor." An independent Quebec, for Dumont, can only be justified, however, if French-Canadians can "prove to ourselves and to others that nationalism is not the introversion we are accused of and that it is simply the courageous acceptance of what we are in terms of our more universal responsibilities": nationalism must be made "one of the indispensable component parts" of "humanism."[23] A humanistic nationalism must be based on "values with a collective appeal, that represent agreement and approval by human groups on a common life-style." Specifically for Quebec those values must condition the "tools of economic growth" and "the broader decision-making processes" so that French-Canadians can "push" themselves "in as contributors of originality in a wider area." Dumont's utopian hope for Quebec is that it become "a testing ground:" "Stuck in the northern half of the American continent, but foreign to America as well," the Québécois might "be able to invent an original form of democracy that springs from their very smallness," a model for the Western world, the "first opening to the universal" of the French-Canadian people. Dumont's thought here recalls that of Ortega, who sought for Spain a more general destiny in modern Europe, and, further back, that of Ernest Renan, the nineteenth-century liberal nationalist, who wrote: "A nation is a great solidarity, created by the sentiment of the sacrifices that have been made and of those which one is disposed to make in the future."

The Bureaucratic Class

Dumont is careful not to fill in the canvas of his humane nationalism with great detail; the work of concrete self-definition cannot be accomplished by the philosopher, who must be content with warning of reifications ("On the one hand we tend to insist too exclusively on rationality in means and ends, and this goes with a virtually exclusive devotion to the rights of individuals; on the other hand, the form of a mythical Quebec moves us to leave aside the conflicts of the interests and groups that belong to our society") and with adumbrating the broad lines of possible development ("generalizing the idea of an experimental society" based on democratic participation). The primary means by which an experimental society might be established is, for Dumont, socialism, which he defines as "an interrogation of the whole of society," an "overall criticism" that guides collective action between the pitfalls of "bogging down in circumstances or limited reformism." Dumont's socialism is deeply Christian and is based upon the dual attitude of the Christian consideration of poverty: there must be "immediate and concrete testimony" before the poor person whom one encounters and also contribution to the "transformation of society," which implies "acceptance of the need" to try to construct "an egalitarian and fraternal society." In light of his analysis of the incoherent society of St.-Jérôme in *L'Analyse*, it is not surprising that Dumont believes that the new middle class, "our young technocracy," should be a major force in effecting socialism: it is "one of the only decision-making groups to embody a fairly precise idea of the general good."[24] A Quebec socialism nurtured within a context of national independence would tailor the state "to the society whose under-development and desire for growth it represents," thereby mediating between "the solid daily humiliations of the French Canadians and the reassuring and abstract generalities of federal pseudo-planning."[25] Dumont believes that "few collectivities have felt as deeply as our own that there is no profound support for human relations but a utopia." Here Dumont appeals again, as he did in his discussion of nationalism, to a special vocation for Quebec, a second "opening to the universal" that would reveal to the rest of the world the essential structures and best promises of social existence.

The nationalist and socialist aspects of Dumont's utopia for Quebec are weighted towards the pole of tradition in his dialectic of traditional and modern societies. Although a humane nationalism and a socialism inspired by the ideal of "an egalitarian and fraternal society" embrace the changes brought about by modernity, they include the appeals drawn from the past to independence for Quebec, national conservation, reliance on the initiating energy and vision of the bourgeoisie (now the "young technocracy"), Christian public morality, and even the unique mission of the Québécois on the North American continent. One might say that Dumont's aim is to convert the present split between unbridled technocracy and romantic nationalism into a "modern tradition," an oxymoron that only becomes intelligible in view of the third element of his utopia, democracy.

Dumont's final appeal is to politics, the medium through which social and cultural diversity might be unified through its self-conscious expression and dialogical conciliation. He grounds democratic politics in the mediating function of speech: "between work and symbols, between rationality and dreams, speech is the way to articulate history and gain mastery over it."[26] In a democratic politics, speech "feeds on the desires and dreams that circulate among men" and helps also to "tame them, subdue them in dialogue and schemes which in turn make possible the political community's existence."[27] Here Dumont applies to Quebec the same pattern of thought that informed his discussion of the convocation of Christians. His "free citizen" and also his model "head of state" must defend their own positions, while "at the same time watching over the renewal of the consensus that allows such positions to be expressed." Democracy is the unifying dynamic, the moral nerve, of nationalism and socialism. But "politics is first of all the recognition of conflicts," "born in violence, of struggles between economic forces, between privilege and enslavement." Its *dédoublement* is to attempt "to introduce a new kind of power and struggle." And in a participative democracy that effort "requires a terrible patience for the bitterness of all to be expressed."[28] That "terrible patience," the undercurrent of utopianism that makes it genuine, the political analogue of "obstinate torment," recalls Dumont's warning to Christians that their struggles will be marked by "much groping and much suffering."

Dumont's reflections on Quebec open on to a consideration of the role of the *penseur*, perhaps we might call him a "practical philosopher," in the present era. As beings who are "condemned to the profane" and whose mission it is to "discover the *a posteriori*" in the full sense of *aletheia*, we (and here Dumont can speak for more than just Christians or Québécois) are invited to engage ourselves freely in the construction of communities of *sens*, of cultures that are coherent yet dynamic "blends of signs," as he calls them in *The Vigil*. The philosopher, acutely aware that we are enmeshed in a flesh that extends beyond our bodies and into the world and our social constructions, issues that invitation and makes tentative moves towards transforming it into the feast of reconciliation itself. But the flesh is discontinuous, the disarticulation of society is expressed in the conflicts of interests and ideologies, and, most profoundly, we wander with "obstinate torment" in a September mood among things that do not seem to respond to our deepest desires. To discover and confer *sens*; that is the promise. To acknowledge and suffer *absence* with "terrible patience;" that is the present demand. In his utopian vision Dumont provides a model for the vocation of the contemporary thinker, who must remain close to the particularities of the flesh and open to the universal, cognizant and respectful of the past, but thoroughly critical and experimental.

Notes

Photo credits: The reproductions of the artistic work of Paul-Emile Borduas were taken from *artscanada*. "The Presence of Paul-Émile Borduas", special issue, December 1978/January 1979, Issue No. 224/225.

1

1. Cited in Gaétan Brulotte, "L'Intraitable," *Possibles* special issue entitled "In search of modernity," Vol. 8, no. 3, Spring 1984, p. 124.

2. *Le Lieu de l'homme: la culture comme distance et mémoire,* Hurtubise HMH, Montreal, 1971, p. 9, hereafter *Lieu.*

3. See Robert Hébert, "Hypothèses laconiques sur un lieu en temps de paix," *La Nouvelle Barre du Jour* (Intellectuel/le en 1984), nos. 130-131, October 1983, p. 114.

4. Allan Wallach, "The Avant-garde of the Eighties," *Criticism,* Vol. 1, No. 3, p. 43.

5. L'Hexagone, Montreal, 1983, pp. 11-12.

6. In "Théorie: la pensée en panne, réinventer la vitesse . . .", *La Nouvelle Barre du Jour,* op. cit. p. 44.

7. Laurent-Michel Vacher, "Intellectuel l'an prochain, même: tentative d'idées simples,"*NBJ,* p. 24.

8. *Ibid.,* p. 24

9. *Essai de sociologie critique,* Hurtubise HMH, Montreal, 1978, p. 178.

10. André G. Bourassa, *Surrealism and Quebec Literature: History of A Cultural revolution,* trans. Mark Czarnecki, University of Toronto Press, Toronto, 1984, p. 86.

11. Georges Vincenthier, *Histoire des idées au Québec, 1837-1980,* vlb éditeur, Montreal, 1983, p. 215.

12. See P.E. Trudeau, "La stratégie de la résistance n'est plus utile à l'épanouissement de la cité," and F. Dumont, "À la jointure de la conscience et de la culture," both in Vincenthier, op. cit. pp. 230, 231, 235.

13. *Ibid.,* p. 236.

14. Carolle Simard, "La culture institutionnalisée: Étude du cas québécois," *Questions de culture,* No. 7, Institut québécois de recherche sur la culture, 1984, p. 152.

15. *La politique québécoise du développement culturel,* Vol. 1 (Perspectives d'ensemble), Éditeur officiel, Gouvernement du Québec, Québec, 1978, p. 48.

16. George Grant, *Lament for a Nation: The Defeat of Canadian Nationalism,* McClelland and Stewart, Toronto, 1970, p. 81.

17. *La politique québécoise du développement culturel,* Vol. 2 (Les trois dimensions d'une politique), Éditeur officiel, Gouvernement du Québec, Québec, 1978 p. 168.

18. Simard, op. cit. p. 159.

19. "Les politiques culturelles, une affaire marginale," *Le Vent de l'espoir 1960-1985,* special supplement *Le Devoir* newspaper, Montreal, n.d., pp. 44-45.

20. Op. cit. p. 150.

21. *Lieu,* op. cit. p. 143.

22. *Ibid.,* p. 161.

23. *Ibid.,* p. 173.

24. *Ibid.,* p. 177, 179, 200.

25. Paul-Émile Borduas, *Refus Global,* in "The Presence of Borduas", a special issue of *artscanada,* December 1978/January 1979, No. 224/225, pp. 19-20.

26. François-Marc Gagnon, "The Death of Signs: Borduas' Last Paintings", *artscanada,* December 1978/January 1979, No. 224/225, p. 51.

27. This is to say, then, that Borduas, with the novelist Hubert Aquin, is one Quebec artist who understood correctly Nietzsche's injunction that art in the age of postmodernism can *only* be a reflection on the disappearance of society into the sign of that which never was.

28. But unlike Fernand Dumont who will short-circuit the interpretation of postmodernism by a leap of faith, Borduas refused any evasion of the crisis of existence signified by "obstinate torment". In the same way that David Cook has said of Camus that he refused the *suicide of the ego,* Borduas rejected the suicide of existence.

29. Gagnon, *op. cit.,* p. 55.

30. Michel Foucault, *Language, Counter-Memory, Practice,* edited by Donald F. Bouchard, Cornell University Press, Ithaca, New York, 1977, p. 35.

31. *Op. cit.,* p. 33.

32. *Ibid.*

33. Everett C. Hughes, *French Canada in Transition,* Chicago: University of Chicago Press, 1943.

34. See especially: Nicole Laurin-Frenette, *Production de l'État et forme de la nation,* Montréal, Nouvelle-Optique, 1978; Gilles Bourque, *Classes sociales et question nationale au Québec 1760/1840,* Montréal, Parti Pris, 1970; and *Espace régional et nation: pour un nouveau débat sur le Québec,* edited by Gérard Boismenu et al., Boréal Express, Montréal, 1983.

35. Guy Rocher, *Introduction à la sociologie générale: Regards sur la réalité sociale,* (Tome 1: *l'action sociale*), Éditions Hurtubise HMH, Montréal, Québec, 1969, p. 1.

36. For a more complete account of the Canadian discourse on communications and technology, see Arthur Kroker, *Technology and the Canadian Mind: Innis/McLuhan/Grant:* New World Perspectives, Montréal, 1984; and St. Martin's Press, New York, 1985. And for an eloquent interpretation of Northrop Frye's contribution to understanding technology, see David Cook, *Northrop Frye: A Vision of the New World:* New

World Perspectives, Montreal, 1985; and St. Martin's Press, New York, 1985.

37. Guy Rocher, *Introduction à la sociologie générale: Regards sur la réalité sociale,* Tome 1: *l'action sociale;* Tome 2: *l'organisation sociale;* and Tome 3: *le changement social,* Editions Hurtubise HMH, Montréal, 1969.

38. *Ibid.,* p. 525.

39. *Ibid.,* p. 190. In what is a clear break with Talcott Parsons' conception of the "enhancement of adaptive capacity" as a basic *evolutionary* strategy in the development of late modern societies, Rocher views adaptation as both domination and creation. "L'adaptation n'est donc pas seulement passive, elle est aussi une forme de créativité et d'innovation".

40. *Ibid.,* "Sociologie et action historique", pp. 526-530.

41. *Ibid.,* p. 158. "En réalité, Comte est déjà 'l'homme de l'organisation'. Il annonce la bureaucratisation de la société industrielle; il prévoit le rôle grandissant des technocrates de l'industrie et du pouvoir politique; plus encore, Comte prend fait et cause en faveur d'une société aménagée suivant la rationalité des planificateurs et des organisateurs. La société industrielle de Comte, c'est en définitive le Plan."

42. Rocher's "general sociology" might, in fact, be viewed as a major attempt at mediating the "wound" in western experience opened up by the rupturing of subject and object in the dialectic of Enlightenment. This is why Rocher concludes his general sociology with a plea for sociology as an "ethical project", both immersed in its object of study and seeking to distance itself from it. See particularly, "Qu'est-ce que la sociologie ?", *Introduction à la sociologie générale,* pp. 522-530.

43. Marcel Rioux, *Essai de sociologie critique,* Hurbubise HMH, Montréal, Québec, 1978, p. 22.

44. *Ibid.,* p. 178.

45. See *Lieu,* p. 39 and *passim.* Also Fernand Dumont, "La culture savante: reconnaissance du terrain," *Questions de culture,* No. 1., IQRC/ Léméac, Québec, 1981, pp. 17-34, hereafter *CS.*

46. *Lieu,* p. 49.

47. *CS,* p. 19.

48. *Ibid.*

49. *CS,* p. 22.

50. *Ibid.,* p. 31.

51. *CS,* p. 32, note 16.

52. Léon Brunschvicg, *De la vraie et de la fausse conversation*, Presses universitaires de France, Paris, 1951, p. 105, cited in *CS,* p. 20.

53. *CS,* p. 33.

54. Dumont concludes *Les Idéologies,* Presses universitaires de France, Paris, 1974, with a call "to enlarge the theory of intellectualization to the dimensions of a sociology" (p. 181).

55. *La Vigile du Québec,* Hurtubise HMH, Montréal, 1971, pp. 195, 233 hereafter *Vigile.* Emphasis added.

56. *Vigile,* p. 223.

57. *Ibid.,* p. 216.

58. *Ibid.,* p. 232.

59. See Judy Steed, "The Unquiet Revolution," *Report On Business Magazine,* May 1985, p. 20.

60. Ernest Renan, *La réforme intellectuelle et morale de la France,* Paris, 1871, *in fine.*

2

1. Fernand Dumond, *Parler de Septembre* (Montréal: Éditions de L'Hexagone, 1970), 11.

2. Fernand Dumont, *Le Lieu de l'Homme* (Montréal: Éditions HMH, 1968), 9.

3. Fernand Dumont, "Pour participer à un dialogue," *Sociologie et Sociétés,* XIV, 2 (Octobre, 1982), 174.

4. *Parler de Septembre,* 50.

5. Fernand Dumont, "La Culture Savante: Reconnaissance du Terrain," *L'Institut Québecois de recherche sur la culture,* 1980, 17-18.

6. *Ibid.,* 18.

7. *Parler de Septembre,* 39.

8. For a discussion of twentieth-century Mexican thought see Michael A. Weinstein, *The Polarity of Mexican Thought: Instrumentalism and Finalism* (University Park: Pennsylvania State University Press, 1976).

9. *Le Lieu de l'Homme,* 11.

10. *Parler de Septembre,* 30.

11. *Ibid.,* 29.

12. *Ibid.,* 30.

13. Fernand Dumont, *L'Anthropologie en l'Absence de l'Homme* (Paris: Presses Universitaires de France, 1981), 9.

14. *Ibid.,* 9.

15. *Le Lieu de l'Homme,* 9.

16. George Grant, *Time as History* (Toronto: CBC Learning Systems, 1969), 52.

17. *Le Lieu de l'Homme,* 9.

18. Fernand Dumont, *Les Idéologies* (Paris: Presses Universitaires de France, 1974), 9.

19. *L'Anthropologie en l'Absence de l'Homme,* 12.

20. *Ibid.,* 9.

21. *Ibid.*

22. *Parler de Septembre,* 64.

23. *Le Lieu de l'Homme,* 13.

24. Gagnon, "Ce curieux produit de culture," *Sociologie et Sociétés,* XIV, Z (Octobre, 1982), 143-144.

25. *Ibid.,* 144.

26. Fernand Dumont, "La sociologie comme critique de la littérature," in Dumont, *Chantiers: Essais sur la pratique des sciences de l'homme* (Montréal: Éditions HMH, 1973), 34.

27. *Ibid.,* 35.

28. *Ibid.,* 46.

3

1. Fernand Dumont, *L'Anthropologie en l'Absence de l'Homme* (Paris: Presses Universitaires de France, 1981), 7.

2. *Ibid.,* 236.

3. *Ibid.,* 314.

4. *Ibid.,* 317.

5. *Ibid.,* 336.

6. Fernand Dumont, "Remarques sur l'enseignement de la philosophie," in Dumont, *Chantiers: Essais sur la pratique des sciences de l'homme* (Montréal: Éditions HMH, 1973), 245.

7. *Ibid.,* 246.

8. Fernand Dumont, *Le Lieu de l'Homme* (Montréal: Éditions HMH, 1968), 125.

9. *Ibid.,* 127

10. Fernand Dumont, "Pour participer à un dialogue," *Sociologie et Sociétés,* XIV, 2 (Octobre, 1982), 172.

11. *Le Lieu de l'Homme,* 125.

12. Fernand Dumont, *La Dialectique de l'Objet Économique* (Paris: Éditions Anthropos, 1970), xii.

13. *Ibid.,* xiii.

14. *Ibid.,* 37.

15. *Ibid.,* 261

16. *Ibid.,* 165

17. Fernand Dumont, "L'histoire à faire, l'histoire à écrire," in *Chantiers,* 53.

18. *Ibid.,* 55.

19. *Ibid.,* 58-59.

20. *Ibid.,* 60.

21. Fernand Dumont, "Idéologie et savoir historique," in Dumont, *Chantiers,* 83.

22. "L'histoire à faire . . . ," in *Chantiers,* 60.

23. *Le Lieu de l'Homme,* 13.

4

1. Fernand Dumont, *L'Anthropologie en l'Absence de l'Homme* (Paris: Presses Universitaires de France, 1981), 30.

2. Fernand Dumont, *Pour la Conversion de la Pensée Chrétienne* (Montréal: Éditions HMH, 1964), 97.

3. *Ibid.,* 112.

4. *Ibid.,* 118.

5. *Ibid.,* 86.

6. *Ibid.,* 168.

7. *Ibid.,* 157.

8. *Ibid.,* 129.

9. *Ibid.*

10. *Ibid.*

11. *Ibid.,* 130.

12. *Ibid.*

13. *Ibid.,* 234.

14. *Ibid.,* 149.

15. *Ibid.,* 211.

16. *Ibid.*

17. *Ibid.,* 212.

18. *Ibid.,* 235.

19. Fernand Dumont, *Les Idéologies* (Paris: Presses Universitaires de France, 1974) 140.

20. *Pour La Conversion de la Pensée Chrétienne,* 234.

21. *Les Idéologies,* 77.

22. *Ibid.,* 9.

23. *Ibid.*

24. *Ibid.,* 170.

25. *Ibid.,* 171.

26. *Ibid.,* 179.

5

1. Fernand Dumont, *Les Idéologies* (Paris: Presses Universitaires de France, 1974), 166.

2. Fernand Dumont, "De l'idéologie à l'historiographie: le cas Canadien-français," in Dumont, *Chantiers: Essais sur la pratique des sciences de l'homme* (Montréal: Éditions HMH, 1973), 89.

3. *Ibid.,* 92.

4. *Ibid.,* 93.

5. *Ibid.,* 100.

6. *Ibid.,* 106.

7. *Ibid.*

8. *Ibid.,* 110.

9. *Ibid.,* 113.

10. Fernand Dumont, "L'étude systématique d'une société globale," in *Chantiers,* 129.

11. *Ibid.*

12. Fernand Dumont and Yves Martin, *L'Analyse des Structures Sociales Régionales: étude sociologique de la région de Saint-Jérôme* (Québec: Les Presses de l'Université Laval, 1963), 6.

13. *Ibid.,* 4.

14. *Ibid.,* 196.

15. *Ibid.,* 147.

16. *Ibid.,* 204.

17. *Ibid.,* 147.

18. Fernand Dumont, *The Vigil of Quebec* (Toronto: University of Toronto Press, 1974), vii.

19. *Ibid.*

20. *Ibid.,* xii.

21. *Ibid.,* 21.

22. *Ibid.,* xiii.

23. *Ibid.,* 50.

24. *Ibid.,* 83.

25. *Ibid.,* 84.

26. *Ibid.,* 102.

27. *Ibid.*

28. *Ibid.,* 116.

KEY READINGS

Fernand Dumont

L'Anthropologie en l'absence de l'homme, Paris: Presses universitaires de France, 1981.

Chantiers: essais sur la pratique des sciences de l'homme, Montréal: Édition HMH, 1973.

La Dialectique de l'objet économique, Paris: Éditions Anthropos, 1970.

Les Idéologies, Paris: Presses universitaires de France, 1974.

Le Lieu de l'homme: La Culture comme distance et mémoire, Montréal: Édition HMH, 1968.

The Vigil of Quebec, Toronto: University of Toronto Press, 1974.

Pour la conversion de la pensée chrétienne, Montréal: Éditions HMH, 1964.

Co-Authored

DUMONT, Fernand, *Idéologies au Canada français: 1900-1929,* Québec: Laval P.U. (Histoire et sociologie Culture 5), 1974.

DUMONT, Fernand, Jean Hamelin & Jean-Paul Montminy, *Idéologies au Canada français: 1930-1939,* Québec: Laval P.U. (Histoire et sociologie Culture 11), 1978.

HAMELIN, Jean, DUMONT, Fernand, *Idéologies au Canada français: 1940-1976,* Québec: Laval P.U. (Histoire et sociologie Culture 12), 1982.

DUMONT, Fernand, MARTIN, Yves, *Imaginaire social et représentations collectives,* Québec: Laval P.U., 1982.

DUMONT, Fernand, MARTIN, Yves, *L'Analyse des structures sociales régionales: étude sociologique de la région de Saint-Jérôme,* Québec: Les Presses de l'Université Laval, 1963.

Poetry

Parler de Septembre, Montréal: Éditions de l'Hexagone, 1970.

L'Ange du matin, Montréal: Édition de Malte, 1952.